Adventures
of an
Advertising
Woman

*May all your adventures be
happy ones.*

*Best,
Jane Maas
Feb '86*

Adventures of an Advertising Woman

JANE MAAS

ST. MARTIN'S PRESS
New York

Design by Janet Tingey

Library of Congress Cataloging-in-Publication Data

Maas, Jane.
   Adventures of an advertising woman.

   1. Maas, Jane. 2. Women in the advertising industry—United States—Biography. I. Title.
HF5810.M33A36   1986   659.1'092'4   [B]   85-25022
ISBN 0-312-00683-7

First Edition

10 9 8 7 6 5 4 3 2 1

This is for Kate and Jenny,
and in memory of Margaret,
as well as for the many women who have taught me
about achievement and, more important, compassion.

Contents

Acknowledgments   ix

A Day on Madison Avenue   1

Life Before Advertising   15

Close Encounters With David Ogilvy   43

Of Shoes and Ships and Flooring Wax,
of Cabbages and Kings   61

P & G & Me   99

The "I Love New York" Experience   116

Wild Animals I Have Known   149

Handmaiden to the Queen   160

Madame President   182

Working and Loving It . . . and Loving   203

Acknowledgments

I am grateful to Tom Dunne, best of editors, and his assistant Pam Hoenig at St. Martin's Press; and to Lynn Nesbit, best of agents, and her associate Suzanne Gluck at ICM. A host of old friends were kind enough to share memories, read manuscript, make suggestions, and suggest titles. They include: Eleanor Berman, John Blaney, George De Coo, David Crane, Elly and Jock Elliott, Clifford Field, Linda Bird Francke, Charlie Fredericks, Gene Grayson, Pat Hatry, Peter Hochstein, Ron Hoff, X. Houghton, Jud Irish, Brendan Kelley, Ian Keown, Reva Korda, Mary Wells Lawrence, Mike Lesser, John Martin, Charlie Moss, David Ogilvy, Bill Phillips, Joel Raphaelson, Elaine Reiss, Ken Roman, Roberta Salter, Jay Schulberg, Ken Shaw, Bruce Silverman, the late Jack Silverman, Bruce Stauderman, Phyllis Cerf Wagner, and Susan Weston.

Here at Muller Jordan Weiss, thank you to my partners Frank Muller, John Jordan, and Andy Weiss; to Mel Kalfus for his infinite patience in making me computer literate, and to Linda Lisi and Margaret Lord-York for assisting him; to Steve Price and Glenn Davis, who portaged the portable computer back and forth on weekends. Most of all, my gratitude and love to Dolores Zahn, who helped me start the book, and to Jude Halleran, who got me finished.

Adventures
of an
Advertising
Woman

A Day on
Madison Avenue

5:30 A.M. Up to do warmups prior to our jog.

6:00 A.M. Three times around the reservoir in Central Park. Michael, because he's left-handed, goes clockwise; I go counterclockwise. We exchange greetings at midpoint. (Sometimes Michael gives me an affectionate pat on the rear end.)

Michael, an architect and a managing partner of HLW, New York's largest architectural, engineering, and design firm, is clearly the best-looking man on the track. In fact, *Good Housekeeping* recently named him one of the ten best-looking men in New York City!

I use the time, as I do every morning, to make a list of things I want to accomplish today. Then I turn the letters into an acronym so it's easy to remember. This morning's list turns into SAJSTINOPM. "S" for the new business presentation to the Society for Savings Bank of Hartford that begins the morning; "A" for a call to my attorney about Leona Helmsley's lawsuit against me; "J" for a Japanese kite; "S" for lunch with the president of our client Stroehmann Bakeries; "T" for outlining a speech on more efficient uses of one's time; "I" for interviewing an account executive; "N" for a new business brochure, and so on.

7:11 A.M. Shower, shampoo, apply conditioner.

7:14 A.M. Do warmdowns to stretch muscles after jogging. (Recently scolded by doctor.)

7:24 A.M. Back into shower to rinse out conditioner.

7:25 A.M. Brushing, flossing, massaging-gums routine. (Recently scolded by dentist.) I tried briefly to combine brushing with warmdowns, but only dripped toothpaste on feet.

7:30 A.M. Blow dry. Life was simpler in the days before Leona made me keep my hair longer. All I needed then was a comb and a towel.

7:45 A.M. Remembering what my old boss Harry Salter of "Name That Tune" always advised about dressing for presentations, I pick out a bright pink suit to wear for the new business pitch.

7:50 A.M. Handwrite a note to a client saying I will be delighted to help his niece find a job in advertising.

7:55 A.M. Leave note for housekeeper. "Please buy bluefish, tomatoes, and interesting lettuce."

8:01 A.M. The doorman calls up. The car is here. Michael is still in his bathrobe, drinking coffee, reading the *Times*. I ask if I may have it drop me off at my office and return for him. "Beg," Michael commands. It's part of our routine. I hold my hands before me like paws, and pant. Michael says, "I'll see you at seven."

8:04 A.M. Sal, our doorman, opens the door to the car. I climb in, say hello to Glenn, Michael's driver. Only two years ago, my normal route was via the Lexington Avenue subway. A car with a driver is the nicest possible perk. It's like a dishwasher: Once you have one, you wonder how you ever managed without it.

8:05 A.M. I note my weight in the little notebook always in my purse and write, "I hope we do a good job on the Society pitch today. Oh, I want that account! I really want that account!" I never ask God to intercede for new business. There are some things, after all, that we have to do ourselves. At moments like this, though, it's a close call.

8:06 A.M. Scan Phil Dougherty's column to see what's new in the world of advertising. There's a photograph from a commercial about to run for a fast-food chain. Phil quotes the head of the chain and the president of the advertising agency. They both emerge sounding fatuous, a bit pompous. Phil pokes a little gentle Irish fun at them. A friend from one of my two advertising alma maters, Wells, Rich, Greene, has been elected a senior vice president. I jot a reminder to myself to write a note of congratulation.

8:25 A.M. We arrive at 666 Fifth Avenue. I take the elevator to the fifteenth floor, walk through our elevator lobby, and use my key to enter the offices of Muller Jordan Weiss, a twenty-five-year-old advertising agency, where I'm president.

8:32 A.M. There's already a stack of mail on my secretary's desk. I walk through her office and into mine, a room that always makes me feel sunny. It's white and uncluttered, the walls covered with Milton Glaser's "I Love New York" posters. Yesterday's daisies are still bright.

8:35 A.M. The caterer is setting up for the Society for Savings breakfast in the larger of our two conference rooms. They have forgotten the linen napkins. Will we settle for paper? We will not. They get on the telephone, assure me the napkins are on the way.

8:45 A.M. Back in my own office. Dolores Zahn, my assistant, arrives with coffee for both of us. She takes one look at my out-box and whinnies. Dolores and I have been together for five years. The whinny tells me she knows I worked into the wee hours last night, so she will have to work like a horse today.

8:50 A.M. I type out the acronym from the morning jog and hand it to Dolores. "I must, must, *must* not leave here today without doing every one of these. What's the name of that Japanese store on Lexington Avenue? Did you make the lunch reservation at '21' for 12:30?"

Dolores shoots me a "So it's going to be one of *those* days" looks. "It'll all get done, one way or the other," she soothes. The way she says "all" betrays the fact that she is thoroughly and completely Irish. Dolores will kill for anyone she loves, a select group that happily includes me.

"I made the reservation at '21' as you very well know, since you stood right here and heard me make it. And I don't have the foggiest idea in the world where that Japanese store is, nor do I care, but by the time you get out of your meeting, I'll know."

8:57 A.M. Why lose three minutes? I type a note to the new senior V.P. at Wells, Rich, Greene and cross that off my list of things to do. The first "cross off" of the day. Good.

9:00 A.M. The team presenting to Society for Savings assembles in the conference room. We are all wearing blue Nike running shoes; it's part of the pitch. Our creative director informs me he is losing his voice. I tell him it's all in his mind, recommend tea and lemon. Is all the equipment plugged in? It is. Are the agendas at each place? They are. The linen napkins arrive. A good omen.

9:10 A.M. I station myself in the Muller Jordan Weiss elevator lobby to greet our prospective clients.

9:15 A.M. The Society for Savings group arrives. Bankers are punctual.

9:42 A.M. In the conference room, more than halfway through our presentation, we show them the "big idea" that will change their image, cause them to be perceived as the innovative bank they truly are. The line is "Society is on the move!" and we recommend they use a running shoe as their symbol. The television storyboard shows another of our suggestions—that everyone at the bank wear running shoes for the kickoff month of the campaign. I jog in place enthusiastically. The president of the bank listens intently, but doesn't react.

Next, we present a backup idea, removing our jackets and revealing T-shirts that proclaim, "Society made me what I am today!" The president looks startled. Is he afraid we are going to strip further? Does he think we're creative or just weird?

10:15 A.M. We escort the Society group to the lobby. Elliott Miller, the president, is cordial. So are Peter Mulligan and Mary Chase. Todd Ikard, executive vice president, shakes my hand warmly. "I had such a good time I don't want to leave," he tells me. Mary Chase says they have three more agencies to see and will make a decision within ten days.

10:16 A.M. I take the leftover croissants into the bull pen, where the pasteup men have been working like animals to get this presentation ready, and say thank you. Then start what are known around the agency as "Mother Maas's Morning Rounds," sticking my head into some offices, dropping in for a minute or two at others, taking temperatures, sniffing the air.

10:44 A.M. Dolores finds me in the Media Department. Some sixth sense always tells her where to track me down. A NEW BUSINESS CALL! The marketing director of a famous brand of expensive imported cookies is on the phone. She has heard nice things about Muller Jordan Weiss from other accounts for whom we do food advertising. Could we make her an informal little presentation on Friday? Friday would be wonderful. Dolores starts clearing calendars, putting together our "agency capabilities" presentation, with an emphasis on food marketing.

11:05 A.M. Our director of marketing services calls to say he has just heard from Dolores about the Friday morning presentation. That day will mark a first in his sixteen years at Muller Jordan Weiss: two new business pitches in one day. Cookies in the morning, insurance in the afternoon. "Mel," I say, "let's start trying for *three*."

Have we any word on the computer company we presented to last week? Mel and I both want that one badly. "We'll know by the end of the week, I think." We sigh, hang up.

11:10 A.M. Three people need to see me. Dolores threatens she will start giving out numbers. Every one of them says it's urgent. First, one of our best copywriters tells me he cannot work another minute with a certain account executive. David Ogilvy gave this advice to his heads of offices, "Compose sibling rivalries." With the reluctant approval of the copywriter, I invite the account executive to join us. It all turns out to be a misunderstanding; a lost work requisition. They leave arm in arm.

11:16 A.M. One of our senior vice presidents has a new business lead: an airline. We discuss the fact that their search is already public; the list of agencies they are interviewing has been announced. He implores me to call the president of the airline anyway. I do, and am vastly surprised to get right through to him. He is extremely gracious, says he knows me by reputation, and explains they are looking for an agency with international offices in place. I wish him luck and send him an autographed copy of my book, *How to Advertise*.

11:41 A.M. The head of our Production Department needs approval to hire a second traffic director. We agree to start looking. An advertising agency is only as good as its traffic and forwarding staff. For the want of a nail . . .

11:45 A.M. I have exactly one-half hour to get to Azuma to buy a Japanese kite for the grandson of one of our clients, the president of Levolor. It is raining buckets, but Glenn and the car are not available. I grab my trench coat from the closet, get down to the lobby, my head full of new business presentations, reach for belt, discover it's not there. I am wearing Dolores's raincoat. Since she is about eight inches taller than I am, the coat flaps around my ankles. I return, stand in her office looking like Little Orphan Annie, and we laugh. Out again, this time in my own coat, dash to Azuma, buy kite, return. Dripping. Dolores asks, "Why do you keep volunteering for things like this?"

12:15 P.M. Michael calls. "Eight o'clock," he begins. "Claude Rains, Paul Henreid . . ."

"I don't believe it," I reply.

"Ingrid Bergman . . ."

It's one of our games. It means we'll be watching *Casablanca* in bed that night for the 117th time.

Michael is not one for lengthy telephone chats. He signs off saying *"Ciao."* (He is learning Italian with his new Atari computer. When he repeats something properly, it tells him *"Benissimo."*)

12:20 P.M. Dolores tells me she is going across the street to St. Patrick's for Mass, and reminds me that this is a Holy Day of Obligation. I tell her that the priest who instructed me when I converted to Catholicism fourteen years ago never told me about Holy Days of Obligation.

Dolores waves her index finger at me. "Ah, but now you know." She is aware I won't be going to Mass. "I'll pray for you. And that we get the bank."

"Thanks, honey, but don't pray for new business."

12:25 P.M. It's only two minutes from my office to one of my very favorite restaurants, The "21" Club. Michael, as an ex-Marine, knew the late "Colonel Bob" Kriendler, one of the owners. We have been regulars there for years. I greet my client, Pete Wygant, the brilliant, witty head of Stroehmann Bakeries, and order six oysters and a green salad, no dressing. (I bring my own bottle of Walden Farms Reduced Calorie Dressing in a Baggie, and use that. Walden Farms is another client, who makes the best-tasting low-cal dressings around.) Not many restaurants will let you order six oysters and a little salad without sneering.

Jerry Berns, another of the "21" family, stops by the table to thank me for helping his granddaughter look for a job in advertising. I answer, truthfully, that she is a nifty young woman and certain to find a good spot.

Pete and I discuss flying in bad weather, then turn, for the rest of the lunch, to the subject at hand: bread. We talk about the marketplace, trends, the competition, new product ideas. After coffee, we have a brief tussle over the bill. Usually, when entertaining clients on my turf, I win, because "21" doesn't present a bill to me. They mail it later. But Pete Wygant, former hockey player for the Montreal Canadiens, makes it quite clear that *he* was the host of this luncheon. Did I care to wrestle him for the check? I retreat gracefully, and we leave the restaurant, Pete bound for Butler Aviation and his private plane.

1:35 P.M. A whole hour before the phones start ringing again. Rapture. There are eleven telephone messages on my desk. No sense in returning calls now, as most people are at lunch. I shuffle through my in-box. Dolores divides mail into "Business" and "Personal."

In "Personal" there's a warm letter of congratulation from an old friend who heard me deliver a recent speech. I write, in the top margin of her own letter, "Helen dear, The nicest notes come from the nicest people," sign it with love, and put it in the out-box. Dolores will pop it into an envelope. These marginal notes are great time-savers and an easy way to make small, gracious gestures.

Request from an advertising club that I visit and speak. New business never comes from advertising clubs. I scribble in the margin to Dolores, "D: regular regret letter."

Request from the director of Alumni Relations of Bucknell University. He is trying to revive the New York City alumni club. Will I make a speech at their first reception? As an alumna and a trustee, I figure it's my obligation to help, so type a letter accepting. (I type like the wind, using two fingers, on the world's oldest manual typewriter, only on yellow paper. That flimsy yellow stuff is copywriter's paper, meant for rough drafts. Psychologically, it's liberating; it signals the writer that this is a *draft*. It's not meant to be clean, finished copy. I cross out, start over, revise. Then Dolores types the final version.)

Here's the daily report from the executive director of the Governor's Committee on Scholastic Achievement, telling me, as chairman of the annual dinner, how many tables we have sold. We are ahead of last year, but not up to the goal we've set. I add to my "to do" list a reminder to twist a few more arms.

Not much in "Personal" today. I know Dolores has already sorted, discarded anything I don't need to see.

1:45 P.M. The "Business" folder is bulging. On top, where Dolores has carefully placed it so it's the first thing I see, is a letter from the director of communications of the computer company to whom we presented. She says they will let us know their decision this week. I mentally cross my fingers.

Seven or eight conference reports advise of decisions made at meetings held with various clients. One of my first memos after becoming president of Muller Jordan Weiss was to the entire account management staff, asking that I be copied on every conference report. (One account executive replied with a memo stating he did not write conference reports on his account. I sent him back a memo that said "Please start.")

I scan all the reports, discard some, send several back to account executives with handwritten marginal comments. "Why are we changing strategy? Seems dangerous. Pls. explain." "Greg—this is a nifty, crisp conference report." "Margot—conference reports should always have an action orientation. State next steps and the person responsible."

First draft of a marketing plan for our client Imperial Knife, with a note asking for my comments. Into the briefcase. Homework.

Memo from one of my partners, Frank Muller, who encloses a cheese wrapper from a product he's discovered in Vermont. Why don't we find out if they might be in the market for an advertising agency. I write a brief note on my memo paper, "Frank Muller: Am following up on cheese," and put it with the rest of the stack in my out-box.

2:05 P.M. Dolores is back from lunch. She asks about Pete Wygant, reports that St. Pat's was Standing Room Only.

2:15 P.M. Carole Dixon, director of Forty One Madison, the New York Merchandise Mart, and one of my favorite clients, calls, close to tears. The advertisement that appeared in today's issue of *HFD*, listing the names of all the Forty One showrooms open for Gift Market, left out the name of one of the most important tenants. Carole moans; she feels it is her fault. I moan. Dolores, who serves as account executive, moans loudest of all. We agree I will write to the president of the company and apologize. As soon as we hang up, I write the letter, and ask Dolores to send it by messenger. Whose law is it that says if anything can go wrong, it will?

2:30 P.M. The creative and account team who will present to the insurance prospect on Friday meet me to go over the speculative creative work. There are three different campaigns, and we narrow down to two of them. I ask the creative folks to keep thinking. "We need something like the running shoe for Society. Something that will set them apart; position them."

The creatives roll their eyes. Do I realize it's only two days to the presentation? I remind them I used to be a copywriter myself, and *anything* is possible in two days.

3:15 P.M. That meeting took longer than it should. Dolores gives me three telephone messages: Michael Maas; my partner John Jordan; and a name I don't recognize. Dolores tells me he's a Bucknell student. I say, "Oh, hell."

First, Michael. He tells me he has to go to Los Angeles two weeks from Friday. "Remember I told you *I* have to go to Ogden, Utah, two weeks from Wednesday for the Levolor sales meeting?" We agree to meet in Los Angeles Friday night, have dinner in our room at L'Ermitage, and fly home together on Saturday.

"Sexy," I say.

"*Benissimo,*" Michael says. "See you at seven. Sharp!"

"Yes, admiral," I reply meekly.

John Jordan, pipe-smoking Phi Beta Kappa who is chairman of the agency and head of the Monsanto account group, is ebullient. A genetic research company with whom we'd met a few weeks ago has just called to say Muller Jordan Weiss will be their agency. I yelp with delight. They do things like fooling soybean seeds into thinking it's fall when it's still summer.

"Gee, John, if we get the computer business too, we'll really be the 'cutting edge of the future' agency, won't we?"

I call the Bucknell student, a marketing major looking for a job in advertising. Dolores stands over me, her arms folded, eyebrows raised. We have made a pact about this kind of call. I go into the speech Dolores has made me memorize. "I'm terribly sorry, but demands on my time have made it just impossible . . ." The student says he understands and is grateful that I took the time to call back. We hang up. Dolores nods approval and returns to her office.

Guilt overwhelms me. Somebody has to help these kids get started. I call him back and we set a date.

The intercom buzzes. Dolores has heard the conversation. "God help me," she says. "I'm working for a lunatic."

3:45 P.M. My partner Andy Weiss calls from New Jersey, where he is meeting with the Levolor clients. The Japanese kite is a big hit. *And* we sold the storyboard. "Yea, yea," I cheer.

3:50 P.M. Jenny Maas calls from Fordham. Can she have her allowance two days early this week?

3:55 P.M. Jenny's call prompts me to check in with Kate Maas, who works for a search firm that specializes in placing copywriters and art directors. We agree on a date for a mother-daughter dinner the following week, on a night when Michael will be out of town.

3:59 P.M. Dolores tells me the young woman is here to be interviewed for the account supervisor job. I note she's early; a good start. We talk for half an hour. This supervisor will report directly to me, so she'll have to be at ease with very senior clients. My gut hunch tells me Chris will be just that. Any weaknesses? Chris confesses that she doesn't always delegate as well as she could. I grin, and confess to the same weakness. We agree on salary, and I tell Chris I'll check her references, and be back to her by next week.

"I bet you hire her," Dolores says. "Another member of the Irish Mafia."

4:30 P.M. Time for our weekly meeting of the heads of the Media and Creative departments. In most agencies, the creatives don't even know who the media people are! We find these brainstorming sessions often lead to more creative planning. Copy Group head Pat Fagan talks about his idea for Stimorol, "the chewing gum for the rich." He wants to do a magazine ad announcing it is the first chewing gum ever to be insured against loss by Lloyds of London.

Fran Menaker, media director, suggests radio, using talk-show disk jockeys who can deliver the commercial live and invite listeners whose gum has been lost, stolen, or strayed to call in and tell about their experience. We might get some tall tales and a lot of extra mileage. Good idea.

5:05 P.M. A call from the director of communications of the computer company, Susan Gauff. "Hi, Susan," I say. We have become friends during the eight weeks of the new business procedure as she narrowed down to four finalists.

"Hi, Jane." she answers. Her next words are, "I'm sorry." My stomach lurches.

Susan tells me we did a super job and the decision was close, but they have decided on another agency.

"I have a hunch that it was about as hard for you to tell me this as it was for me to hear it," I comment.

"Thanks for understanding that. It was." We agree to stay in touch.

Dolores comes in and hugs me. "I'll pray for that bank."

"No, it's okay," I tell her. "Win some, lose some." She hugs me again, and leaves for the day.

I walk down the hall to our creative director, deciding not to ruin his night's sleep. "Jerry, the bank presentation this morning was fabulous. Full of crackle. Let's hit it on Friday just like that. I think we're on a roll."

Jerry beams. I exit, poke my head back in. "We need another running-shoe idea."

5:45 P.M. Three items left on the "to do" list. Impossible to finish them all. I call my attorney. Leona Helmsley has given her deposition. She was formidable. Formidable! But not to worry. After all, only $10,000 is at stake. I bet Leona isn't worrying.

5:50 P.M. Okay, Jane Brown Maas, stop grieving about the computer company and concentrate on writing the new business brochure.

6:30 P.M. I read over what I've written. Lousy. Might as well make the rounds of the office to see who's working late. The Media Department is there as usual, computers humming. The Levolor team is meeting with the head of Television Production on the Levolor commercial. The Monsanto account folks are doing a marketing plan. Everyone seems pleased to see me. The captain is on the bridge.

6:50 P.M. I walk over to Park Avenue. There's the car, Glenn at the wheel, Michael inside reading the newspaper. He asks me how my day went.

"We didn't get that computer account." Michael pats my hand. "And I didn't get around to writing that speech on how to organize your time better."

"Organize your time better," Michael says.

7:15 P.M. While Michael showers, I read the draft of the Imperial marketing plan, and jot marginal notes.

7:55 P.M. In our nightshirts in the kitchen. Michael makes omelets with Japanese mushrooms. I make the salads. We pour two glasses of white wine and carry the trays into the bedroom.

8:00 P.M. *Casablanca* comes on. Peter Lorre explains to Humphrey Bogart that the letters of transit are worth lots of money. Money? Money?

"Please God," I pray silently, "give us the bank."

Life Before Advertising

My first *real* job in New York was working for a television quiz show, "Name That Tune." Contestants in sneakers vied to be first to run up, ring a bell, and identify a song. The tunes weren't difficult. In fact, the one most often missed was "Stardust." "Name That Tune" had a warmth and charm that made it one of the most popular shows on CBS. The secret lay in the personality of the contestants.

It was my job to interview them, uncover any areas of humor, tenderness, or drama, and if I did, indicate to master of ceremonies George DeWitt where he might probe.

I discovered, for instance, that Benny Reynolds, a cowboy from Montana, tended to answer in monosyllables. So I suggested that George pepper him with questions. It resulted in the following exchange:

GEORGE: Benny, I gather that you're a cowboy.
BENNY: Yup.
GEORGE: And you come from Helena, Montana?
BENNY: Yup.
GEORGE: Benny, do you always talk this much?
BENNY: Nope.

While chatting with a contestant from the Midwest, I asked if she and her husband had enjoyed the experience of breakfast in their room at a New York hotel. "Heck, no," she replied earnestly. "Gus took one look at the menu and said he couldn't take those prices lying down." My note to George DeWitt said, "Ask her about breakfast in bed."

My work with contestants gave me a grass-roots feeling for how Americans talk, and even more important, how they respond emotionally. I have drawn on this knowledge for the rest of my career.

Yet I never intended to have a career in advertising. Theater was always my first choice, journalism my second. During my senior year of college, my mother told me she'd heard that advertising people made a lot of money.

"Advertising!" I sneered. I'd read *The Hucksters* and *Man in the Gray Flannel Suit.* All of us liberal English major types at Bucknell knew about the evils of advertising. "That's the last thing in the world I'll ever do."

When I arrived at Bucknell, I had attained my adult height of exactly five feet, and weighed in at a chubby 122 pounds. I wore my hair (brown in those days) in a long ponytail to allow for versatility in playing different roles. The uniform of the day was skirt, sweater, bobby socks, and loafers. My personality was, and is, relentlessly cheerful; I've never recovered from being a cheerleader.

As soon as I finished unpacking in my room at Bucknell Cottage, the oldest dormitory on campus, on a floor known as "Silverfish Alley," I ran out to get to know people. A distinguished professor of English told me, years later, that on my first morning at Bucknell, I had cordially welcomed *him* to campus. Another professor confessed that he avoided passing me in the narrow halls of the Literature Building. He always feared I would leap at him, like a round, affectionate puppy.

It was Bucknell tradition that early in the semester, certain visible freshmen women would be subjected to a gentle hazing. I had to wear a birdcage on my head, and was marched around campus, blindfolded, singing "The Woody Woodpecker Song." The more I writhed in embarrassment, the more my voice cracked in bad imitation of Woody, the more the crowds of upperclassmen laughed. I loved every minute of it. It was my first taste of theater at Bucknell.

Professor Harvey Powers asked me to be his assistant director for the musical production of *The Vagabond King*. For the next four years, I acted in, directed, or hung around the fringes of every play produced at Bucknell. I played the kid sister in *Our Town* ("Grovers Corners; Sutton County; New Hampshire; The United States of America; the continent of North America; the Western Hemisphere; the Earth; the Solar System; the Universe; the Mind of God"); the ingenue in O'Neill's *Ah, Wilderness!*; Maria in *Twelfth Night*; Mrs. Candor in Sheridan's *School for Scandal*; and my favorite role of all, The Madwoman to Philip Roth's Ragpicker in *The Madwoman of Chaillot*. (Almost thirty years later, Philip sent me a copy of his novel *The Ghost Writer* inscribed, "To the sanest Madwoman there ever was, from her Ragpicker, Phil.")

Eddie Davis (who went on to become president of Broadway's Theater Now) and I codirected *The Student Prince*, the biggest moneymaker of our four years. As a senior I directed Sophocles' *Oedipus Rex*. In many ways, directing was even more satisfying than acting. The director is, emotionally, "on stage" the entire time.

My schedule did not vary. During the daytime I went to classes, wrote occasional articles for the college newspaper, *The Bucknellian,* acted in skits for the Bucknell radio station, attended sorority meetings, worked on the yearbook and eventually became editor. Nights, until the 11 P.M. curfew for women, and every weekend, we rehearsed for a play. I did my homework between midnight and dawn.

If I hadn't been known on campus for all that extracurricular activity, I would probably have been labeled a "greasy grind." During my four years at Bucknell, I received an A in every course, with the exception of Algebra 100. Even now, when I think of it, I cry. I went into the final exam with an F average and would surely have flunked, without the help of a friend majoring in psychology. The night before the exam, she put me under hypnosis, and told me I would have a photographic memory of everything I studied in the textbook. I went without sleep, walked up the hill next morning with delicate little steps so as not to joggle my mind, and got an A on the exam and a C in the course. I do not remember taking the exam or anything about algebra.

Senior year, almost inevitably, I bit off more than I could chew. In addition to being president of the drama club, editor of the yearbook, actress, and director, I signed on for the English honors seminar (*Beowulf* to Virginia Woolf) *and* the French honors seminar (Proust!).

The hard-core theater people arrived on campus a week early, in time for freshman orientation. We vied with the organization that provided our major opposition on campus, The Christian Association, in signing up freshman members. *The Bucknellian* ran an editorial, "Who's Getting the Freshmen? Cap & Dagger or God?"

By Christmas, I was so busy that I came back to Bucknell after just two days at home. The women's dorms were closed for the holiday, so I slept on a cot in the yearbook office, much to the horror of the night watchman, who didn't believe young women should carry on like that.

By the beginning of the last semester, I was staggering with fatigue. My advisor gave me the bad news. I needed one more three-credit course. I elected Early English History, which met every Monday, Wednesday, and Friday at 8 A.M.

I never got to it. Not once. I just slept through every class. In early May, my head cleared long enough for me to sniff danger. I went to the professor, whom I knew, and told him I had been ill. The darling man, known as Creampuff, expressed concern. He had taught both my parents when they were Bucknellians. And he knew my scholastic standing as well as I did.

I presented him with my own translation from the medieval French of a description of the Battle of Crécy, never before translated. It was dedicated to him.

The night before the exam, without benefit of hypnosis, I stayed up and opened the history book for the first time. Creampuff gave me an A. But whenever I am anxious about anything, I dream I am back at Bucknell, taking an exam for a course I have never attended. A psychiatrist friend once told me this is a very common anxiety dream, in which the subconscious substitutes for a real concern one that is totally unreal. I told him there is nothing unreal about my dreams at all.

So I graduated *summa cum laude,* with honors in French and English literature, a Phi Beta Kappa key awarded during junior year, and the clear conviction that I was Golden Girl. (I wore that Phi Beta key for years on a chain around my neck, until a more sophisticated friend suggested diamonds were better.) Career choices? The theater or journalism. Not advertising. Never advertising. My only brushes with advertising at Bucknell occurred when I realized that we needed to sell ads to help pay for the printing of the yearbook and the programs for each play. I summoned the respective advertising managers, responsible for handling this distasteful chore. "Sell more ads than last year." It was my first marketing strategy. Then I stayed away until the money was counted.

After Bucknell came a Fulbright Scholarship to the

University of Dijon, to study modern French theater. The university system in France is extremely thorough and tends to concentrate on one area, unlike American survey courses, which gallop across centuries. We began on playwright Paul Claudel in October, and when school ended in May we were still with him.

Dijon became famous for two reasons during my year there. The mayor, one Canon Kir, invented a way to persuade his citizens to consume more of the locally produced currant syrup, cassis. The good mayor simply added it to his wine, and a new apéritif was born. It became known worldwide as a Kir.

The other commotion in Dijon was created by one of its tiny hotels. The promotion-minded proprietor decided to increase occupancy and garner publicity by connecting the bathroom taps to wine vats. The hot tap gave you red, the cold white. The French thought it a charming idea and came to drink a glass or two. Then word reached the nearby American army base, and the G.I.s checked into the hotel, smuggled in steel drums, and returned to camp the next day with enough *vin ordinaire* for a regiment. The owner sadly closed down his pipeline.

We five Fulbrighters in Dijon hoarded our monthly government checks for travel. Two went skiing. Two made gastronomic tours of Burgundy. I went to London or Paris to gorge on theater. I skimped on meals to buy theater tickets, and lost ten pounds during my year in France. Not svelte, but improving.

I had crushes, successively or simultaneously, on: a French professor; an American corporal who brought me Aunt Jemima pancake mix; an American student at Oxford; and an English journalist. But my true love of that year was actor Jean-Louis Barrault. Still dreaming of a theater career, I saw every play he appeared in.

Next, Cornell University and a fellowship in theater arts. The first play of the season was my old favorite,

Twelfth Night. A stage-struck engineering student, Gordon Davidson, was playing one of the minor roles, Curio. He was awful. A few days after the last performance, we had a heart-to-heart talk. "Gordon," I said candidly, "you better stick to engineering. You clearly just aren't cut out for the theater."

Gordon Davidson soon made headlines as one of America's most innovative directors. He was the driving force behind Los Angeles's Mark Taper Forum, and created hits such as *Children of a Lesser God* and *The Shadow Box.* So much for advice.

I wrote my master's thesis with one hand and job-application letters with the other. It seemed there were no openings in the theater, so I sent a barrage of resumes to every New York newspaper and magazine. The few who bothered to respond at all sent form letters of regret.

It took a telephone call to Time Inc. to discover there was an opening, even if it was a temporary one. The secretary to the advertising director of *Life* was going on vacation for two weeks. I passed the typing test, got through the dictation test by writing feverishly in longhand, and was hired.

In the mid-fifties, *Life* magazine was at the peak of its success and kingpin of Henry Luce's empire. The advertising dollars that flowed into its glossy four-color pages were the envy of the publishing world.

During my two weeks there, I witnessed one of the constant skirmishes between advertising and editorial. One of the editors planned a photo essay on the bums in the Bowery. Advertising pleaded that it be dropped, afraid it would offend the many liquor advertisers. Editorial won. It always did. Henry Luce made it clear that his magazines were run by the people who wrote them. His title, after all, was not publisher, but editor-in-chief.

I once spent a few moments alone with Mr. Luce (we called him "Henry the Great") but it was completely by accident. The elevator starters in the Time-Life Building were under firm orders to send Henry Luce up to his penthouse office on the thirty-second floor *alone*. I didn't know this, and one morning, close to being late, ducked under the starter's arm, and found myself facing those famous beetle brows. He was just as startled as I was. We ascended in silence. Luce stared heavenward. The doors opened, and he stalked out. Recently, I read in his biography that Luce, a pious Presbyterian, used those moments alone every morning in the elevator to pray!

Before the vacationing secretary returned, Personnel summoned me. They had a permanent job opening. Would I like to be secretary to the woman who ran the entire Office Services operation for Time Inc.? It seemed a long way from the smell of grease paint or even printer's ink, but I needed the money and said yes.

In the man's world of Time Inc., Ruth Goodhue was one of the few powerful women. Another was Content Peckham, the only woman listed on the masthead of *Time* as an editor. She supervised the sixty women researchers. The lines were clearly drawn in those days; women researched the stories, men wrote them. To me, however, the researchers lived glamorous lives, traveling all over the world to dig out facts, and having ultimate control over the writer's story. In his quest for accuracy in journalism, Luce had developed an elaborate checking system. The researchers had to put a dot over every single word in the finished essay. If there were any words the researcher could not verify, they went dotless until the writer changed them. (Despite this system, everybody was aware of the editorial biases that flowed from Luce. While I worked there, *Time* helped to defeat the candidacy of Adlai Stevenson when he ran for President in 1956.)

Other famous women at Time Inc. were photographer Margaret Bourke-White and, of course, playwright, Congresswoman, and Ambassador Claire Booth Luce. Word went out when either one was on the premises, so we could gather and gawk at these, our own celebrities.

Ruth Goodhue ruled the twenty-second floor of the Time-Life Building. Whatever anyone wanted, from a paper clip to a new building, emanated from Office Services. It was an especially busy time, as Luce had just decided he wanted a more modern headquarters. He put his son, Henry III, known as "Hank," in charge of the project. Hank coordinated everything through our office.

Hank Luce popped in often, but the Great Man summoned people to his penthouse office. When his secretary called, everybody jumped. One day, she called just as Miss Goodhue was going out the door to lunch with a friend. My boss was usually serene under pressure, but her hands trembled as she powdered her nose. "Cancel lunch and send my apologies," she told me. "Harry Luce wants to see me."

I loved working for Ruth Goodhue, but envied the more romantic world of the journalists who worked on *Time*. Their week ran from Thursday through Monday night, when the magazine "went to bed." When everything was wrapped up, there was a Lucullan—or Lucian—feast, catered by the posh Louis XIV restaurant across the street.

The director of communications came up with a bright idea that let me get a little closer to the journalistic action. Weekends, as the magazine headed toward final deadline, were usually frantic, and often there weren't enough people free to take down fast-breaking stories as writers called them in. The Communications Department installed devices that answered the telephones automatically and taped the writers' reports. Some human beings were needed to monitor the tapes, and I volunteered.

One quiet Sunday, the telephone rang. It was one of *Time*'s most famous writers, a big, gruff man who was the epitome of tough reporter. He was calling from the

Southwest, at the scene of the worst disaster in airline history, the collision of two tourist-packed commercial flights. He was dictating his story rapidly, but his words were absolutely unintelligible. I interrupted him, explaining he could not be understood.

"Why the hell not?" he asked.

I was afraid to tell him it was because he was crying.

It was heady, working at Time Inc. Great writers, great photographers, a benevolent organization that paternally doled out benefits. It was whispered that nobody was ever fired. We heard that those in high places who fell from favor were assigned to offices on the twenty-sixth floor, reserved for souls in Purgatory. There, they were given nothing to do. Usually, they got the hint. Some people left of their own accord. Among the stars who defected were Theodore White and Emmet Hughes, both because of disagreements with Luce.

As secretary to the head of Office Services, I rated my own small office with a window that overlooked Rockefeller Center. (It was to be years before I had an office that splendid anywhere else.) We watched the seasons change under our noses: the lilies at Easter, the tables and umbrellas that sprouted in summer, the ice skaters and the lighting of the Christmas tree. There was no air conditioning in the Time-Life Building, so we closed on any summer day that the temperature went over ninety degrees. When it did, we all cheered and rushed home to our own hot, non-air-conditioned apartments.

Mine was on West 70th Street, just off Central Park West, on the third floor of a brownstone. The rent was $130 a month, and three of us shared it: Barbara, a fellow Fulbrighter teaching high-school English; Anita, a pretty redhead who studied with Martha Graham by day and worked as a hat-check girl at the Versailles nightclub at night; and me. We had a big living room, a biggish bedroom, and a kitchen that really didn't exist; it was just equipment hidden behind ancient shutters. We thought our home was divine.

My days were Office Services, my weekends were journalism, but my evenings were still devoted to theater. I saw a lot of Ed Davis, the only one of the Bucknell drama gang who had actually ended up with a paying job in the theater. Eddie was working for a production company and wangled us free tickets to just about every good show on Broadway. Some nights, we baby-sat for stage manager Max Allentuck and his wife, actress Maureen Stapleton, who lived right across the street from me. They were a spirited couple. Max fidgeted in the living room one evening, checking his watch, yelling for Maureen to hurry up. She finally made her entrance.

"Comb your hair," Max commanded.

"I combed it," Maureen countered.

"What with? A fork?" Allentuck riposted. Eddie and I wondered how such a turbulent marriage could ever last. It didn't.

One of the writers I'd gotten to know during my weekend telephone stints introduced me to a favorite *Time* hangout, The Absinthe House on West 48th Street, long since torn down. This restaurant brought together my two favorite worlds, journalism and theater.

Phil Silvers, starring in America's most popular television comedy, "Sergeant Bilko," was there, trading jokes with Buddy Hackett and radio's Henry Morgan. (Morgan was a hero to the Time Inc. crew because of the way he always put down advertising on his radio show. We heard that Kellogg had fired him after he put on earmuffs to drown out the sound of the "Snap Crackle Pop" of a Rice Krispies commercial.) Robert Preston stopped by when he was in New York and made my heart beat faster.

The writers included Richard Condon, then a movie publicist with dreams of *The Manchurian Candidate* in his eyes, and a young investigative reporter for *Collier's* magazine, Peter Maas. Peter is the author of such best-sellers as *The Valachi Papers, Serpico, King of the Gypsies,* and *Marie.* He is better known to me now as brother-in-law.

Two cartoonists were part of The Absinthe House scene on occasion: Al Capp and George Baker. Capp, rich and famous after years of "Li'l Abner," was witty, charming, and reputed to be one of the great rakes of the Western World. He invited me to join him at his suite in the Waldorf one night for "a quiet bite to eat," but I was too scared to accept, so I never found out.

George Baker, who created the classic GI cartoon character "Sad Sack" during World War II, was a slim, shy man who resembled his creation. One night he came to a party in our apartment, and sat off in a corner, doodling. It turned out he had just conceived a new character, "Little Sack." I still have that drawing, made on yellow scrap paper, yellower with age now and faded, but just as precious.

Upstairs at The Absinthe House, a world-class game of backgammon for high stakes went on nonstop, long before backgammon had become popular. I asked Peter Maas not long ago if all the people who are now famous writers were up there playing.

"No," he said gravely. "The famous writers were all at their typewriters in their offices, which is why they became famous writers. The people who played backgammon upstairs all day are the great unknowns."

Suddenly, I was back in show business, via the wonderful, wacky world of television. I was walking down Broadway one night with two Bucknell friends, both unemployed actors. We agreed that all they needed was just one break; just to be "discovered." A woman stopped us, looked directly at me, and asked if I would like to be a contestant on a quiz program. I obviously looked like the kind of person who jumps up and down and squeaks with enthusiasm. I was; I still am. They selected me as a contestant on "Name That Tune." My musical knowledge was scanty. I won a few hundred dollars, shook hands with the M.C., and departed. A few days later, my telephone rang. The producer offered me a job.

Harry Salter had a great nose for public relations. I think he hired me because he sensed I shared it. Even more important, Harry's wife, Roberta Semple Salter, had grown fond of me while I was a contestant. I had listened, fascinated, to her tales of growing up in America as the daughter of evangelist Aimee Semple McPherson. She knew I was a good listener who seemed adept at drawing people out. What better qualities for one who might interview contestants, ferret out funny anecdotes and foibles of human nature?

Harry and Roberta Salter were a genius couple. Harry understood exactly what the nation wanted in its entertainment. He had created "Stop the Music" back in the heyday of radio. Fred Allen wrote of that program in his autobiography. The heart of "Stop the Music" was a telephone call to a randomly selected home, anywhere in America. If the residents were listening to the program, they had the chance to identify the "Mystery Melody" for a huge jackpot. The show became a national phenomenon. Nobody went anywhere on Sunday nights or listened to any other station, afraid the telephone might ring. Fred Allen, in the unhappy time slot opposite "Stop the Music," took out an insurance policy to woo back listeners by guaranteeing them the jackpot money anyway, should a listener be called during *his* program.

Roberta Salter added another dimension. "Sempie" had watched her famous mother captivate throngs. She knew that certain simple themes touched even the most cynical Americans. Religion was one. Love of family, respect for courage, patriotism, patient endurance are some of the others.

"Name That Tune" hired me on a part-time basis; I

worked three nights a week. Monday and Wednesday nights, we interviewed prospective contestants at Steinway Hall. The "headhunters" brought them in; then, if they were considered possibilities for air, they came to me for interviewing. Tuesday nights the show came on live at 7:30 P.M. *Live!* No editing, no chance to do a section over again. It was everything you've ever read about the days when television was young.

One of our big challenges was getting off the air on time. George DeWitt had a big crush on actress Linda Christian, widow of Tyrone Power. He kept hoping the contestants would end their game early enough for him to sign off by singing "Linda." Harry Salter's philosophy was to keep the action going until the last possible second. Poor George never got to sing more than one line of "Linda," and his courtship foundered.

After the show, I'd go back to CBS (then at 485 Madison Avenue, "the most famous address in America") and call the hometown television stations and newspapers of the winning contestants.

For almost a year, I worked full time at Time Inc., part time on "Name That Tune," and Saturdays and Sundays at *Time* magazine monitoring writers' telephone calls. There wasn't much time for romance, but I was beginning to think I would never meet somebody I loved who would love me back.

The Salters, the production staff, and, most of all, the contestants made "Name That Tune" the hit show it was. Many of our contestants went on to fortune; some of them to extraordinary fame.

One of our most famous contestants was John Glenn, a Marine Corps jet pilot. George DeWitt asked him if he believed man would ever go to the moon. "Yes," John grinned. Then, a full six years before he would become the first American to orbit earth, he added, "Even more important, I believe he'll come back."

John had just broken the world's record for supersonic flight from coast to coast, rattling some windows in the process. He gave the nationwide audience one of its first lessons in how fast it felt beyond the sound barrier. "Think of some place that's about ten miles away from your home. Okay, you're off." John checked his supersonic watch. "One second . . . two seconds . . . three seconds. You're there!"

The format of "Name That Tune" had two contestants run up and ring a bell to vie for the opportunity to identify a song. The winner then went on to a "Golden Medley" of songs mailed in by a home viewer. If the contestant named seven of them correctly in thirty seconds, he or she returned the following week to be joined by the home viewer. The partners worked as a team in the possible five-week march of the "Golden Medley Marathon" toward a $25,000 jackpot.

John Glenn's partner was little redheaded Eddie Hodges, who was spotted while on the show by the producer of Broadway's *The Music Man*, starring Robert Preston. Eddie went from our show to Broadway, to television specials, and to movies like *A Hole in the Head* with Frank Sinatra.

Eddie, then in fifth grade, once explained that he was having no luck in his courtship of a little girl in his class. That outwardly tough Marine, Glenn, was sympathetic. "When I was in fifth grade, Eddie, I had such a crush on a beautiful girl in my class, I thought I'd never get over it."

"But you got over it, right?" Eddie nodded, accepting sage advice.

"Wrong," John said solemnly. "I married her." The show's director quickly turned a camera on Annie Glenn in the audience.

Little Eddie's grandfather was a Baptist preacher. John Glenn is a devout Presbyterian. We discovered John and

Eddie had in common good voices and the knowledge of lots of rousing old gospel hymns. One they treated us to came straight from the Chautauqua circuit: "This Train Is Bound for Heaven, This Train."

I followed John's career as he became one of the first seven men chosen to be astronauts, orbited earth, was elected to the Senate, and ran for a Presidential nomination. Eddie Hodges seems to have vanished from sight. Perhaps he just grew up.

Another contestant whose appearance on "Name That Tune" led to fame was Leslie Uggams, then a lanky fifteen-year-old, already with a glorious adult singing voice. One of Harry Salter's great talents was his ability to spot star quality, and he saw it in Leslie. He taught her to sing with simplicity, without unnecessary gestures. One night she stopped the show with "Scarlet Ribbons." The telephone in the office rang all next day. One of the callers was Mitch Miller, producing and starring in "Sing Along with Mitch." He wanted Leslie for a guest appearance. She became a regular on his show and grew up into stardom.

One of my favorite contestants was Trudi Lee, who had mailed in a list of tunes from her small town in Kansas, hoping to win perhaps a few hundred dollars. Divorced or widowed (she was reluctant to discuss the subject), Trudi was gaunt and battered from trying to run a farm alone. When faced with a choice between buying fertilizer or replacing several missing teeth, Trudi opted for fertilizer. Her first appearance on "Name That Tune" must have revived national memories of the dust bowl.

Trudi and her partner, a diminutive German waiter named Emil, were on their way to winning the $25,000 jackpot when the show went off the air for its regular summer hiatus, eight weeks of rerun highlights. Harry Salter, who tried to hide his benevolence, without fooling a soul, persuaded Trudi to stay in New York all summer, while he paid somebody to take care of the farm.

He sent Trudi to his own dentist and had her teeth fixed. He sent Trudi to his doctor for vitamin pills and a weight-gaining regime. And he sent to Kansas for Reuben Keil, a widower who owned the farm adjacent to Trudi's. Reuben and Trudi had been in love for years, but were too burdened by their own debts to want to burden the other.

"Name That Tune" came back on the air in September, and as Trudi appeared on the screen, the audience gasped. She was transformed. Trudi looked especially radiant because, right after the show, she and Reuben were to be married.

George DeWitt announced that fact and, on impulse, invited Reuben up on stage to say a few words. Harry Salter raised his eyebrows at me. We both had reason for concern. Reuben was shy to the point of speechlessness in ordinary circumstances. What would he do facing a TV camera?

George asked Reuben his philosophy of marriage, and Reuben said simply, "Marriage is sort of like a farm. The more love you put into it, the better harvest you'll reap."

Trudi and her partner won $20,000 that night. "New York has been so good to us," Trudi said, "that we'd like to invite everybody to the wedding." She gave the name of the little church in midtown where the ceremony would take place. Viewers from Brooklyn, the Bronx, and Queens leaped into their cars. To our amazement, by the time we reached the church, it was full of well-wishers, who wanted to whisper "Bless you" to Trudi and Reuben.

The following week, just at the climactic moment when Trudi and Emil were about to guess the songs for the big jackpot, the screen went dark. We had been preempted by Adlai Stevenson, who appeared on CBS for a nationally televised campaign speech.

The switchboard at 485 Madison lighted up with calls of protest. I telephoned Stevenson headquarters and persuaded them to release a statement. Associated Press picked up the human interest story, and "Name That Tune" made papers all across the country. The candidate apologized to Trudi and Reuben, who represented three things he held dear: "newlyweds, Kansans, and above all, Democrats."

Well, Trudi and Emil did win $25,000, and the Keils returned to Kansas. About a year later Trudi wrote to say that being on "Name That Tune" was the most exciting event in her life, next to her pig winning first prize at the county fair.

Another unexpected moment came when Mrs. Gus Jueneman, a midwestern housewife, won $5,000 during her first appearance, but declined to return the following week to try for $10,000. Her church at home was having a retreat. George DeWitt didn't seem to know what a retreat was. "It's okay," he soothed Mrs. Jueneman. "We can get you out of it." Mrs. Jueneman was protesting vigorously that she didn't *want* to "get out of it" as we went off the air in confusion.

The staff huddled after the show. How would we handle this unprecedented problem? Roberta Salter ended the debate by reminding us that every churchgoer in America would rise in wrath if we made Mrs. Jueneman forfeit her chances. Harry Salter asked Phil Silvers, whose show followed us on CBS, to pinch-hit for her with her partner, Louie Brugnolatti. Phil and Louie gave us one of our funniest programs ever, and Phil happily handed over his share of the winnings to Mrs. Jueneman.

Louie ("Call me Lulu") Brugnolatti was the quintessential New York cab driver, and a dead ringer for comic Lou Costello. For years after his stint on the show, I never knew when a certain yellow cab would pull up beside me, and a voice would yell: *"Hey, Jay-nee!"* It was part of the game for me to yell back, just as loudly, *"Hey, Lulu!"* Then he'd bundle me off to my destination free of charge, help me out of the car, and give me a big hug. One morning many years later, David Ogilvy watched this performance as Lulu dropped me off in front of Ogilvy & Mather. "My dear," said David, "you have such interesting friends."

Because of the unknown quantity of the write-in contestants, we often had some surprises. One was a lovely high-school student with an unpronounceable name, who turned out to be the great-great-granddaughter of the King of Siam. Another was the famous old vaudevillian Pat Rooney, who had written in, simply from the boredom of retirement, as P. Rooney. Appearing on "Name That Tune" gave Pat a new lease on life. At the age of eighty, he performed one of his old tap-dance routines, ending with a fling that Baryshnikov would have envied. The audience gave him a standing ovation. Reading Pat's obituary less than a year later, I wondered if his last performance was perhaps his greatest.

A redheaded Irishman won the Golden Medley one night. When his partner showed up the following week, she turned out to be a beautiful lieutenant in the Israeli Army, visiting the United States. They went on to win $25,000. At the end of their last show together, the Irishman's elderly father, with a brogue straight from County Mayo, came up to present the lieutenant with a shamrock she could plant on her return to Israel. He gave her the old Irish blessing: "May the road rise to meet you, may the wind be always at your back, and may the good Lord hold you in the palm of his hand."

Interesting tidbit for trivia collectors: The most outgoing, enthusiastic contestants came from Oklahoma. Kansas, not Texas, was a close second. Anyone under ten almost automatically made a good contestant. Our three-star ratings also went to: mothers with more than seven children who were cheerful and hoped for more; men and women in all branches of the service, especially those who were cheerful and planned to reenlist; men and women of the cloth, who were expected to be cheerful and to stay the course.

"Name That Tune" made headlines another time when a young but̤ ̤er was on the program. Joey spoke with such affection and enthusiasm about his cuts of meat ("good skin tone, plump in the right places, lean in the others"), that Harry Salter, in another fit of benevolence, decided Joey should cease to be an apprentice and have his own butcher shop. We found an inexpensive little store on Ninth Avenue, and Harry paid the first month's rent.

One night toward the end of the show, George DeWitt revealed the big surprise to Joey and the nationwide audience. The band played a fanfare, the stagehands trooped in with a huge sign proclaiming JOEY'S MEAT MARKET, and the audience stood to cheer.

The only one not responding was Joey. He seemed sheepish. George, Harry, and I became apprehensive as he cleared his throat. He thanked everybody for everything they'd done. He sure thought it was terrific, but he really didn't want to be a butcher. Ever since he was a little boy, he'd had his heart set on another career.

George DeWitt asked him what that was.

"George," said Joey the Butcher. "I always wanted to be a florist."

The newspaper headlines next day read: "Historic quiz show first: Contestant turns down prize!"

Harry let the month's rent ride on the Ninth Avenue store, and changed the sign to read JOEY THE FLORIST. Last time I looked, Joey wasn't there. I hope he grew so prosperous he had to move to another location, one he had always fancied. Floral Park.

In the fall of 1956, Harry Salter asked me to leave Time Inc. and join "Name That Tune" full time as assistant producer. I left the world of journalism without a twinge of regret or a backward glance.

Harry was paying me $200 a week, more than most American men were making at the time. (The income-tax expert at H&R Block who prepared my return whistled in approval. "Pretty big bucks for a little girl.")

It seemed time to leave the West Side. I told Barbara and Anita they would have to find another roommate, and rented an apartment in a spanking new apartment building on East 46th Street. It was called Executive House; a status name. Mine was the cheapest apartment in the place, one room with a doll-sized kitchen and bath. I read all the designer magazines, papered one wall with Japanese-style wallpaper to set off a "dining nook," bought a Castro convertible and an early American reproduction dining room table and chairs, unfinished, to save money. I never got around to finishing them.

I was paying rent of $135 per month, more than my parents had ever paid in their lives. And I was terribly lonely.

Peter Maas, an Absinthe House acquaintance from the old Time Inc. days, called on a Friday night in February 1957 to ask if I were free for dinner the following evening. These were the days when a young woman of marriageable age sat home on Saturday night with the lights out rather than admit she was dateless. I told Peter that I was busy.

"Too bad," Peter said. "My kid brother, Mike, is coming in from California for the weekend. He's a lieutenant in the Marine Corps."

"I'll break my date," I said. "It's the patriotic thing to do."

Michael Maas arrived the next evening to pick me up, resplendent in his uniform, with the extra gold braid accorded to a general's aide, and a swagger stick. We went on to an evening of drinks and dinner, followed by jazz and stingers, my introduction to that lethal concoction. I invited him back to Executive House for an early-morning snack. Michael says that the inside of my refrigerator looked like a pair 'ng by Dali. It contained a bottle of champagne and one egg. We scrambled the egg, drank the champagne, Michael asked me to marry him, and I accepted. It took me six months to get him to repeat the offer again, sober.

I flew to the Marine Corps base in San Diego in March to visit Michael, on the pretext of hunting for contestants. He had asked me, in one of the frequent letters we exchanged, if I shared his passion for bullfights. I wrote back, fibbing, that indeed I did, and we marveled at the happy coincidence. Then I rushed to the library and read all the bullfighting literature I could lay my hands on, including Hemingway's *Death in the Afternoon*. I figured I could fake it, but no amount of reading prepared me for my first *corrida* at Tijuana. When the first bull hit the first horse, Jane Brown from Jersey City fainted dead away. It may have delayed Michael's proposal by at least four months.

Michael wrote in April or May that he would finish his tour of duty in the Marine Corps on July 15, and asked me to join him on a trip through Mexico for a month. Despite the gloomy predictions of my mother, who warned me that men never married women who went off to Mexico with them, I went.

We started off from San Diego and drove across the desert in a twenty-year-old car with no air conditioning, then on down the west coast of Mexico and across to

Mexico City. Vultures hovered over the car, and lizards scrambled up and down the walls of ancient hacienda hotels. I felt any couple who could get along under those circumstances had a good chance of making it together for life.

In Mexico City, soothed by the cool wines and violins of Les Ambassadeurs restaurant, Michael asked if we could get married as soon as we returned to New York.

"Yup," I said. Benny Reynolds could not have been more succinct.

This turned out to be the best decision I ever made. Michael appears to agree. As I write, we are about to celebrate our twenty-seventh anniversary.

We didn't realize until we were back in New York City in mid-August that we faced certain complications. Michael, a Roman Catholic, had been in the service for three years and so belonged to no parish for publishing the traditional "banns of marriage." And I was best described in those days as "sort of a Presbyterian." Michael's parents asked the advice of their old friend, Elmo Roper. Elmo, who knew just about everyone in the world, said a friend of his could probably handle this unusual situation. He introduced us to Father George Ford, pastor of the small Corpus Christi Church at Columbia University. Father Ford, a friend of Eleanor Roosevelt, was well ahead of his time liturgically. To the horror of the Establishment, he was celebrating guitar masses long before Pope John XXIII and Vatican II declared them a good idea.

Father Ford married us in the chapel of Corpus Christi. We really didn't need a honeymoon, since we'd just returned from Mexico, so we settled for one extravagant night at a posh Connecticut inn, Stonehenge, where Michael had worked as a busboy during his high-school days. Only one thing marred his triumphant return. Stonehenge was hosting a thoroughbred dog show that weekend. There were more poodles in residence than guests.

Kate Maas was born two years later, on Christmas Eve. She was tiny, sweet, and bright, with blond hair and big blue eyes; an accurate description of Kate today.

This was the third Christmas of our marriage, but we'd never had a Christmas tree. Michael felt they lacked aesthetic appeal. The only holiday decorating we did in our little apartment on East 91st Street was the hanging of three tear-shaped silver pendants, severely Danish modern. Since I come from a family that trims trees with balls, cranberries, and popcorn, Christmas without a tree had seemed rather forlorn, but Michael's sensibilities came first.

Christmas morning, I heard a strange, swishing sound coming toward me down the corridor of New York Hospital's Maternity Ward. Michael arrived with a little tree, complete with lights and ornaments. We still have those ornaments, and our trees have become larger every year.

Since I had begun my pregnancy overweight at about 110 pounds, my obstetrician had kept me on a strict diet. After Kate was born, I weighed in at 100, a weight I've maintained ever since. The mother of a Bucknell friend, who hadn't seen me since the days when I was thirty pounds heavier, met me at a party one night. "Goodness," she asked her daughter in alarm. "Has Jane Brown been through some wasting illness?" It was one of the nicest compliments I ever heard.

Kate entered the world just as all the quiz shows left it. The game-show industry was a small one, so we knew that many of the others were rigged. They would keep contestants on week after week, as long as the Nielsen ratings showed they were drawing audiences. As soon as the ratings slipped, the contestant would be asked a question the producers knew he couldn't answer. Simple as that.

The scandal blew up around Mark Van Doren, son of the famous literary family. He had stayed on for weeks and weeks as reigning champion of the show "Twenty-One." Van Doren confessed to the fixing; so did contestants from other shows such as "$64,000 Question" and "Tic Tac Dough."

Since the premise of "Name That Tune" was "songs you've known all your life," we wanted our questions to be easy, not esoteric. I was interviewed by *Look* magazine, which published a long article certifying "Name That Tune" an honest show. Other quiz shows were taken off the air. "Name That Tune" was the last survivor.

Then Congress invited the heads of the three networks to Washington. They decided to present the legislators a schedule utterly devoid of quiz programs. The music stopped.

Harry Salter kept a small staff on salary to develop a new game. He hired my friend and classmate Ed Davis to help. One of our ideas was a spin-off of Harry's own "Stop the Music," using film clips instead of tunes. We named it "Stop the Camera."

Contestants watched film on various subjects, never knowing when it would stop and they would be asked a question about its content. We convinced NBC to produce one pilot show. The best moment was a film of Winston Churchill during the London blitz, telling his countrymen, "I have nothing to offer but blood . . ." The film stopped. The in-home telephone contestant was sure she knew the words that followed: "Blood, sweat, and tears." The exact Churchill words are, of course, "Blood, toil, tears, and sweat."

"Stop the Camera" proved to be an expensive proposition. Researching and editing film cost far more than doing the same things with music. We abandoned the project. Eddie Davis went back to the theater, while I stayed on with Harry Salter.

Harry soon made his comeback as producer of a show on ABC, "Yours for a Song." He promoted me to the rank of associate producer. The young ABC executive who supervised the show was Chuck Barris, who went on to Hollywood and created shows including "The Newlywed Game" and "The Gong Show."

For master of ceremonies, Harry reached out to the man who had emceed the television version of "Stop the Music," Bert Parks, better known as emcee of the Miss America Pageant.

"Yours for a Song" lasted for two years, a respectable run. Sensing its demise, I had begun putting out feelers for another job.

A producer and director of television commercials, Bert Lawrence, knew that Exxon (then still Esso) was looking for cultural programming that would be good for the company image. We created for them "Esso World Theater," a series of one-hour programs on the culture of various countries in which Esso did business.

I wrote the scripts for most of the shows. My favorite was for England, "Puritan versus Cavalier," which starred Sir Ralph Richardson. The program on Greece starred Katina Paxinou, with Robert Graves as host. The hour about Japan featured segments on Kabuki, Noh, and Puppet Theater, and was narrated by the venerable Japanese actor, Sessue Hayakawa.

Another marvelous show was filmed in India. For one segment, we persuaded director Satyajit Ray to create a mini-film which he titled *The Kite*. We also planned to film some famous and erotic cave drawings. Esso had severe qualms about the "GP" rating of these drawings. After many calls between our office and the continuity clearance people at the networks, I sent the following cable to director Robin Hardy in New Delhi, "Breasts okay; fornication out."

I never got to join any of the glamorous film excursions

to England, Japan, India, or elsewhere. I was expecting our second child, who the obstetrician confidently predicted would be a boy. He could tell by the heartbeat rate, he said. We named him, well in advance, Patrick Michael.

The baby was born just before midnight on November 21, 1963. It was immediately apparent that we needed a different name. We had another girl.

The nurse who wheeled me into my room at midnight was an enthusiastic guide. "This is the only room on the maternity ward with a three-window view of the river and its own private shower," she told me. "It's the room Jackie Kennedy had when Caroline was born."

The next afternoon, John F. Kennedy was assassinated in Dallas. My own feelings were expressed in a letter from Elmo Roper. "I am so sorry for you," he wrote. "How difficult to be experiencing such joy when the world is in mourning."

Few people visited. Michael did, of course, and we watched the incredible events of the weekend unfold on television: the lying in state, the murder of Oswald, John Kennedy, Jr., saluting the coffin, Jacqueline Kennedy and the leaders of the world going on foot to the funeral mass.

We also tried to come up with a name for "Baby Girl Maas," who was clearly quite a person, even at the age of one day. She was born full of enthusiasm, energy, and charm, qualities she hasn't lost.

Michael and I couldn't agree on a name. Eddie Davis offered a suggestion. "What was the name of the heroine in *The Lady's Not for Burning*?" It was a Christopher Fry play we had performed together at Bucknell.

"Jennifer," I shot back. A terrific name. Unusual, too. Who else had a baby named Jennifer? Michael approved. Some years later, when we began to realize we had chosen the most popular name of the decade, I reread the play in question. The heroine's name was Jennet.

Our housekeeper, Mabel, met me in the lobby of the hospital. I handed Jenny over and went to the office. I was proving a point back then, saying women didn't need to stay home after having babies. Today, I suggest to my pregnant friends that they take some period of time off, even if it is just a month or two. Infancy is such a precious time and is gone so quickly.

The one "Esso World Theater" devoted to America was filmed in New York, so I did participate in that. It starred George C. Scott and Colleen Dewhurst, then still husband and wife, and William Daniels, soon to appear as Dustin Hoffman's father in *The Graduate*.

One segment was the scene at the grave in *Death of a Salesman*. Colleen Dewhurst, as Willie Loman's widow, gave one of the great performances of her career. At the end of the last take, the stagehands applauded. George C. Scott looked at Colleen, made his famous cud-chewing motion, and nodded solemnly. I gather it is his highest accolade.

Despite all manner of critical acclaim and international awards, "Esso World Theater" didn't perform well in the ratings. It was so elitist, I suspect the only people watching it were the director's wife and my parents. Esso regretfully canceled plans for the following year.

I was about to look for another television job, then thought again about the crazy hours that prevented me from being with my family, about the job insecurity, about the competitive jungle of the television industry. I decided to seek a more *gentlemanly* profession. I selected advertising.

Close Encounters
With David Ogilvy

Since "Name That Tune" was broadcast live, we often had live commercials on the show. The performers ranged from a serious man in a white coat who looked like a doctor (against the law today) to adorable children singing about corn flakes. The actors were accompanied by battalions of advertising-agency people: copywriters, art directors, producers, and account men. They had pretty easy lives, I thought, being responsible for creating just one little minute, while I had an entire thirty-minute program to contend with. And they appeared to make quite a lot of money, almost as much as I was making in television.

So, on the advice of some friends in advertising, I put together a portfolio of speculative advertisements, with Michael assisting as art director, and wangled an interview at Ogilvy & Mather.

David Ogilvy was already a legend on Madison Avenue. He had created the Man in the Hathaway Shirt with the eyepatch; Commander Whitehead for Schweppes Tonic; Titus Moody for Pepperidge Farm bread. Ogilvy & Mather and Doyle Dane Bernbach were considered the two best creative agencies in the United States. Some instinct led me first to 2 East 48th Street, the offices of Ogilvy & Mather.

Joel Raphaelson, then associate creative director, looked at my book. "I suppose that like everybody else you'll want to work on packaged goods," he said, "since that's where the money is."

"Yes," I replied with certainty. "What are packaged goods exactly?"

They are most products sold in packages, from soup to soap, and are usually assumed to demand more marketing and strategic skills from the advertising people who work on them than do towels or knives or tourism. This assumption is false. It takes clear strategic thinking to sell any product. Packaged-goods people, however, continue to be more in demand, more revered, and generally better paid than other worker bees.

Joel sent me for a second interview with Copy Group head Gene Grayson. Bearded, intense, Gene flipped through my meager portfolio of ads and storyboards, pausing occasionally to grunt, "You've got a good headline buried down here in the body copy." We talked for a while, and I fled.

The next day, Gene surprised me by calling to offer me a job as junior copywriter in his group. I hesitated, thinking maybe I was crazy to start at the bottom of a profession I knew nothing about. "Let me think about it, Mr. Grayson."

"Listen, you redheaded fink, get yourself over here next Monday. I am going to teach you everything you need to know about advertising."

I went to Ogilvy & Mather, and Gene kept his promise. From the first day, he was my champion, as well as the most exacting teacher for whom I have ever worked. Gene taught all his creative people to "go for the jugular," and involve the emotions of the viewers. "Make them laugh, make them cry, make them mad, but for God's sake, make them feel something."

My starting salary was exactly half what I had been

making at the end of my television career, but more than many beginning copywriters were paid. My office was a tiny cubicle without a door. Later, I tried to give it more charm by hanging a "curtain" of Japanese bamboo strips across the doorway. This decor prompted one account man to comment, "I'll come in, but I won't go upstairs." Michael came to pick me up at the office one evening, and the bamboo promptly vanished.

A few days after starting work, I met David Ogilvy. The agency was small enough for him to make a point of meeting new people, especially copywriters, whom he considered the *creme de la creme*. David's habit was to drop in on people in their offices, as he believed it terrified them to be summoned to the presence chamber. Even more terrifying was the experience of looking up and finding that awesome, red-suspendered figure in my doorway. (Happily, the bamboo strips were not yet in place.)

I leaped to my feet and introduced myself. "I'm Jane Maas, your newest copywriter." D.O. looked past me to the blank sheet of yellow paper in my typewriter. "Well, newest copywriter, start writing." Then he exited, only to reappear a second later to add, "Welcome."

Another former copywriter at Ogilvy & Mather, Ian Keown, now a well-known travel writer, wishes somebody would compile an anthology of people's introductions to D.O. His, he recalls, left him shaken.

Keown, a young Scotsman, had spent his apprentice years working on copy in Holland and the United Kingdom. He worshiped David Ogilvy from afar, so when he made his way to New York and was actually hired, he felt it a dream come true.

The copy chief escorted him to the elevator, and there stood D.O. himself. Introductions were performed. "David," the copy chief said, "I'd like you to meet our new copywriter. Another Scotsman."

David digested this information, then inquired, "What part of Scotland?"

"Greenock," Keown replied.

"Oh, good God," David said, looking down his nose, "the *west* coast!"

Despite this inauspicious beginning, Ian Keown reports that D.O. invited him to write copy on the important new KLM Royal Dutch Airline account, and on British Travel, one of his pets.

A copywriter fresh out of college, Eleanor Berman, remembers David Ogilvy appearing in the doorway of her office on her first day, and telling her she looked like a nice young girl. He said the previous occupant of that same office had also looked nice, but he never got a chance to find out, because she never said anything in meetings and now she wasn't around anymore. Eleanor says she started talking and hasn't stopped.

Newly arrived copywriter George De Coo was sent to David's office to introduce himself. D.O. wasn't there, but on the table were a hospitable cup of tea and a plate of cookies. De Coo drank the tea and ate the cookies. D.O. materialized and growled like Papa bear, "Somebody drank my tea!" De Coo feared his career was over before it had begun.

David often relied on graphology, and still believes in it, although his partners have persuaded him not to use it as a divining rod for creative powers. He also forms swift first impressions. One of his creative heads, Francis X. Houghton, recalls interviewing a man for a position as Copy Group head. It was about the fifth interview, and X. was prepared to hire him. David entered the office, and X. introduced him to the candidate. David left, but beckoned urgently from outside the doorway. X. went into the corridor to confer.

"For God's sake, you're not going to hire that man, are you?"

"Do you know him?" Houghton asked.

"My God, you ass, look at his handkerchief."

"What?" asked X. in bewilderment.

"He wears his handkerchief the way Harry Truman does!"

Ogilvy & Mather was peopled with bright and wondrous people. Copy chief Clifford Field, an English gentleman and a superb writer, stood out. He wrote one of the most beautiful advertisements of all time, for British Travel. The photograph was the interior of Westminster Abbey. The headline read, "Tread softly past the long, long sleep of kings." (Another copywriter of the Ogilvy school, Bob Marshall, later wrote an advertisement asking for contributions toward the restoration of the Abbey. The headline was "Westminster Abbey is falling down. If this leaves you unmoved, do not read on.")

Also roaming the halls of Ogilvy & Mather were a number of ambitious young account men destined to become presidents of major New York advertising agencies. (Phil Dougherty once commented in his column that Ogilvy & Mather is a great training ground for agency presidents.) They included: Bill Phillips and Ken Roman, both of whom would rise to the presidency of Ogilvy & Mather itself; Charlie Fredericks; Bob James; Bob Savage; Abe Jones; Norman Goluskin; Tom Lawson; Mike Lesser; Dick Costello; John Martin; Richard Seclow; and Wilder Baker. Ray Trapp heads an agency in Dallas, Dave Weiss one in Boston.

D.O. was everywhere. He read every scrap of copy and every storyboard before submission to a client, and it was common to receive a piece of one's own copy back with a comment written in red ink. By his own order, D.O. was the only one at the agency allowed to use red ink; messages from him stood out, as he intended they do. David scribbled terse marginalia. I received two notes from him early on. One said, "Good work." The other said, "Dreadful."

Joel Raphaelson received a note about the tardiness of a certain project. D.O. wrote that he had still not seen anything on the such-and-such project. "You started work on this 93 days ago. Longer than the gestation period of a PIG!"

Every advertisement, no matter how small, mattered to David. X. Houghton, as a copy cub, had worked on an advertisement to appear in a Pakistani newspaper. The client required that some thirty points be made about the product, and X. jammed them all in, knowing it was an awful ad, but thinking, after all, nobody would see it, except in Pakistan. He left the copy on his desk.

Next morning, he saw the familiar red ink in the margin. D.O. wrote, "This is an advertisement written by a man who has heard advertising described, but has never actually seen an advertisement."

Reva Korda, whom David calls "a brilliant copywriter" was the most senior woman in the agency, and when I first arrived, the only woman officer. David discovered Reva when she was writing copy for Macy's. He read an advertisement he liked, called Macy's, found she had written it, and offered her a job on the spot. He often used this method to discover writing talent. Gene Grayson was sitting at his desk one day at another agency, when his phone rang. "This is David Ogilvy," said the caller.

"Yeah," said Grayson. "And this is Abraham Lincoln." He hung up.

The phone rang a second time. "This really *is* David Ogilvy." David had seen a commercial he liked, traced it to Gene, and wanted to hire him.

There were not many highly placed women at Ogilvy & Mather in those days. Those who were reaching middle management were doing it in Creative, Traffic, and Personnel areas. There was no woman management supervisor, and I don't recall that any was an account supervisor.

David had a firm rule against nepotism, one that he states in *Confessions of an Advertising Man*. "Whenever two of our people get married, one of them must depart— preferably the female, to look after her baby." Joel Raphaelson, as a young copywriter, had become engaged to a fellow copywriter at the agency, Marikay Hartigan. D.O. was almost apologetic that one of them would have to go. He tried to find some graceful solution. "You know," D.O. told Joel, "some years ago we had a very senior creative person who was living with our head of production. There wasn't a thing we could do about it. We have no rules against living in sin!"

D.O. thinks quite differently about women now. And certainly, Ogilvy & Mather has long been in the forefront of identifying and promoting exceptional women. More than half of entry-level account management people today are women. Many have reached top management.

David urged his creative people to broaden their horizons: go to the theater, read books, magazines, newspapers, and, above all, advertisements. He wrote a memo in the 1950s that is a collector's item, and I am indebted to Peter Hochstein, now associate creative director of Doremus, for a description of it.

"David suggested to the entire staff that the infant medium of television had a promising future, with important implications for the advertising business. He acknowledged that the stuff being broadcast was absolutely awful, and that TV sets themselves were a nonstatus symbol that created severe home-furnishing problems. Those were the days when a ten-inch television screen came encased in what seemed to be a cubic mile of mahogany cabinetwork.

"So D.O. offered a helpful solution to his $50-a-week

copy cubs and $200-a-week senior writers as to where they might hide their television sets to avoid social embarrassment.

"'I keep mine in the wine cellar.'"

One sin David would not tolerate: *boring* advertising. Clifford Field treasures a note from D.O. about a freelance writer who shall be nameless. "This copy like everything BLANK writes is flat, banal, jejune, pedestrian, dull, commonplace, lifeless, grey. No life, no guts, no enthusiasm, no personality. Let's stop paying money for cold porridge." Field adds, "As a new writer at Ogilvy & Mather, I shivered."

Words were D.O.'s chief weapon in his battle for charming and persuasive advertising. He told me once that he wrote at least one hundred headlines for any given advertisement, every one containing the name of the product and its "promise" or consumer benefit. He then showed them to other creative people whose judgment he trusted.

His most famous headline is, of course, the classic for Rolls-Royce, "At Sixty Miles an Hour, the Loudest Noise in This New Rolls-Royce Comes From the Electric Clock." He admits that he once used the word "obsolete" in a headline, only to discover that most readers didn't know what it meant. He confesses to using the word "ineffable" only to discover he didn't know what it meant himself.

Jock Elliott, now chairman emeritus of Ogilvy & Mather, once wrote a ten-minute talk on the agency's "Clean Up New York" campaign. He sent it to David with a request to "Please improve." David changed *one* word: from *people* who litter our streets to *barbarians* who litter our streets.

Jock thought, "Glory be! Only one word changed. I've made it at last." But the headline of the story in the next day's New York *Times* was "Barbarians Litter Our Streets."

D.O. believes in the Scottish proverb "Hard work never

killed a man." In his principles of management, he states, "The harder our people work, the happier and healthier they will be."

He assumed his staff would work as hard as he did, and was genuinely amazed by one copywriter who did not. "Do you know that every day at exactly five o'clock, BLANK gets up from his desk, puts on his hat and coat, and *goes home*?" Long pause to let it all sink in. "Think of the extraordinary *self-discipline* that takes."

David often cites the words of Mies Van der Rohe: "God is in the details." Bill Phillips, now chairman of Ogilvy & Mather, tells about a big presentation to their new client, General Foods, just after Phillips joined the agency in 1959. The presentation was scheduled for Monday morning. Phillips went to the office Sunday evening to be sure the charts were ready, and to rehearse his part. D.O. was in the office, worrying about the meeting. He persuaded Bill to help him scour the agency to select chairs that matched, and arrange them in his office. They spent over an hour on the chairs. Phillips says, "His concern over practical details convinced me that he not only had his eyes on the stars, but his feet on the ground as well."

One day, D.O. visited the General Foods plant in Hoboken where Maxwell House coffee was made. The aroma of roasting coffee filled the air. "Does Maxwell House coffee taste as good as it smells?" His investigations into the link between aroma and taste led to a successful campaign for Maxwell House.

Confessions of an Advertising Man is the most popular book on advertising ever written. Anyone who has read it knows that David Ogilvy believes in rules; guidelines for what usually works and what usually does not. The Creative Department was summoned with regularity to attend "Magic Lantern" presentations. These were slide shows with rules and examples of good and bad advertising. They included, "How to create advertising that sells," the first of the Lanterns; "How to create food advertising that sells"; "How to advertise travel"; "How to create financial advertising that sells"; and many more.

Linda Bird Francke, who left Ogilvy & Mather to write the "Lifestyle" column for *Newsweek,* and subsequently became a leading feminist writer, once startled David by being in the barber chair (Ogilvy & Mather housed Emile the barber), when D.O. arrived for his haircut. Emile was too charmed by the bright, miniskirted young copywriter to realize she had preempted David's appointment.

After the next Magic Lantern presentation, David invited Linda into his office to ask her what she thought about it. "I think that Lantern was terribly boring," Linda said. "But I think *you're* terrific." David seemed mollified.

The substance of the "Magic Lanterns" appeared in the form of advertisements for Ogilvy & Mather. The last few lines made it clear that the ads were new business tools. "Ogilvy & Mather has developed a specialized body of knowledge in what makes for success in advertising food products, tourist destinations, proprietary medicines and many other products. But this special information is revealed only to clients of Ogilvy & Mather." Did it work? You bet!

David has become more mellow about his rules, but in the old days, woe betide the creatives who broke them. Ron Hoff, now executive vice president of Foote, Cone & Belding, offers the following anecdote.

"When Merrill Lynch was at Ogilvy & Mather, I always regarded it with a kind of proprietary interest. In any event, there was an important ad in the works, and we wanted to make it sort of 'special' looking. So we had a big, dramatic picture with one narrow column of copy running down the side. The art director then did a bold and daring thing. He suggested putting the headline at the *bottom* of the ad, so the column of copy spilled right into the headline. I approved the ad, and the client really liked the layout.

"When David saw it, he challenged me to find the number of stories in the New York *Times* that had the headline at the *bottom* of the story. I had to admit I couldn't find many. None, to be exact. He was obviously disgusted with my judgment, but the ad went through and into production.

"As it turned out, the ad was tested by the client when it appeared. It tested very well indeed. High readership. High seen/associated. High in all critical areas.

"I couldn't resist letting David know the good news. I sent him a memo with the test results. Not gloating, mind you, just the results. I had too much respect for him to gloat. But I must admit I did feel pleased.

"A few days passed. Then, the memo came back, as I knew it eventually would. David's fine script was to be found in an upper corner of the memo. 'Dear Ron,' it said, 'your test scores are very good, but think how much better they would have been if you had put the headline where it belonged.'

"I realized he had me. Once again."

Another of David's rules then was that humor did not sell products. So he hated my "Crying Plumber" for Liquid Drano. The plumber, seated in his truck, broke down as he discussed the virtues of this new drain cleaner. Finally, he burst into tears and wailed, "New Liquid Drano keeps your drains so clean you may never need a plumber!"

Sales for new Liquid Drano took off, but D.O. did not change his mind. I was surprised to learn that he selected it as one of the commercials to show during his speech at the annual meeting. The entire staff of Ogilvy & Mather was gathered.

"I loathe this commercial," he said. In my seat in the

back of the auditorium, I froze. "But it *works*. That is the secret of good advertising. We are not here to win awards. Or to be complimented at cocktail parties. We are here to sell our clients' products. Jane Maas has done that and I congratulate her."

I violated another of his rules in a storyboard for Start, an instant orange breakfast drink. I forget now what rule it was. He invited me to his office to discuss the plight of Start, whose sales were sliding.

I had done my homework, and gave him my complete analysis of the problems. Start was packaged in a tiny cardboard can, and consumers perceived the price as high. Also, unlike the successful Tang, it could not be made by the glass, but only by the pitcherful. "And that's our problem, Mr. Ogilvy," I concluded.

He gave me a conspiratorial smile. "The problem with Start," he confided, "is something I have been worrying about for years. It tastes like *tangerine* juice!"

In addition to loathing stupidity and sloth, D.O. cannot tolerate untidiness. He checked the offices after hours, and left notes if displeased. Bill Wright found such a note from D.O. one morning. It read: "Bill, if you don't clean up this pigsty, you belong outside with the rest of the cattle." Bill cleaned up his desk and soon became head of the San Francisco office of Ogilvy & Mather.

David urged us all to use his client's products. He considered it simply good manners. So we bathed in Dove soap, brushed with Aim toothpaste, began our days with Maxwell House or Maxim coffee, ate Pepperidge Farm bread spread with Imperial margarine, and deodorized our homes with Glade air freshener. Not all of us could afford a Mercedes, but David forgave that.

Every December, David presided over the annual meeting in his made-to-order Sears, Roebuck suit. (He was often on the list of America's best-dressed men.) When he announced that, yet again this year, every man jack of his employees would receive a $100 bonus, D.O. raised his arms high in benediction. This annual ritual never failed to receive a standing ovation. At least it never failed during the twelve years I was there. I always led it.

In 1965, the annual meeting was astir with the news that David was stepping down as chairman of the board. What would his new title be? "I am assuming the proudest title there is in advertising," he declared. "I will be listed in the employee directory as David Ogilvy, copywriter."

Jock Elliott, the new chairman, rose to give a speech. He imagined himself at a cocktail party that very evening, in conversation with a stranger who asked him what he did for a living. Jock would reply that he was in advertising. The imaginary conversation continued, with the stranger asking what agency, and Jock replying Ogilvy & Mather.

"And what do you do at Ogilvy & Mather?" the stranger would ask.

"Actually," Jock would say with a self-deprecating *moue*, "I'm chairman of the board."

"And what is David Ogilvy? Queen of the May?"

Like many men of genius, David has his eccentricities. Food is one of them. Although he began his career as a chef at the legendary Hotel Majestic in Paris and is a recognized gourmet, he cares little for food much of the time. Once, a group of bright young *wunderkind* carefully selected from international offices was invited to join D.O. for dinner at one of the tonier New York restaurants. The maître d' asked D.O. solicitously what he would care to order. "Grape Nuts," said David, impatient to get on to a discussion of advertising. The maître d' blinked, then apologized that, alas, the restaurant had no Grape Nuts that evening. Would Mr. Ogilvy select an alternate?

"Corn flakes," said David.

The rest of the diners at that table all ordered corn flakes too. It was a brief but memorable evening.

Soon after I became a vice president of Ogilvy & Mather, I invited David to be my guest at a celebratory luncheon. He accepted. I chose a good French restaurant for the occasion. As we entered, David spotted a big silver tureen, which contained the specialty of the day. He picked up the lid, stuck his head deep into it and inhaled the perfume of the dish.

The maître d' rushed up saying sternly: "Sir, you can't do that!"

David removed his head from the tureen and turned to the maître d', who instantly recognized his famous guest. He proffered a spoon. "Mr. Ogilvy, perhaps you would care to taste?"

On a trip to an out-of-town client, D.O. was served a sadly overdone steak. He summoned the waiter. "Has the hotel burned down?" (David declares this anecdote fiction. He *likes* overdone steak.)

A great dream of his came true shortly after I joined Ogilvy & Mather. He opened an agency cafeteria where we could all eat inexpensively and, even more important, exchange ideas. He and I stood next to each other in the cafeteria line. "Stay with me," David implored. "You know *everybody*! How do you know so many people when you have been here such a short time?"

As we approached the cash register, David signaled me. "Do you have any money?" he whispered. Like royalty, D.O. traveled without a wallet. I paid for his lunch: $1.17. Like royalty, D.O. never paid me back.

Another of David's eccentricities is fear of flying. Even if Cunard and the *QE II* had not been his clients, he would have preferred to cross the Atlantic by water. Inevitably, D.O. was aboard the *QE II* when she was hijacked. This experience did not change his mind about flying.

In 1984, I attended a luncheon of the Magazine Publishers' Association at which D.O. was guest speaker. He explained that he had asked to speak before luncheon was served, as he was leaving for San Francisco in one hour, *by train.* I wondered whether there was anyone in the audience from one of Ogilvy & Mather's most important clients, TWA. A rare instance of David violating his own rule about using clients' products.

David is also terrified of elevators. One of his partners remembers boarding the elevator with David on the ninth floor of Ogilvy & Mather at just 5 P.M. one evening. As it descended, it stopped at every floor to admit more passengers. D.O. was gradually shoved to the rear. By the time the elevator reached the fourth floor, the car was a sheer wall of humanity. The doors opened, and an enormously fat woman tried to force her way in.

From the rear of the elevator came a distinctive British voice. "For God's sake, don't let her in. She's too heavy. We'll CRASH!"

My favorite memory of D.O. isn't about advertising, but about David himself. He knew Michael and I were vacationing in France with our daughters in an area not too far from his home, and invited us "to dine and sleep" at his château, Touffou. We crossed a moat, drove across the pebbles of a former jousting yard the size of two football fields toward a Mercedes parked in front of a door. From inside came the clatter of a Telex; David was keeping in touch with all Ogilvy & Mather offices around the world.

Michael and I were put up in The King's Chamber, the huge central room of the eleventh-century keep. Kate and Jenny slept in the beautiful Renaissance wing. David was pleased to have as guest an architect who would fully appreciate the glories of Touffou. He took Michael on a tour that covered every inch of the place. Touffou had been declared a "national treasure" and therefore demanding of special treatment by special artisans when repairs were needed. David grumbled that every time the roof leaked, it took *his* national treasure to repair it.

D.O. was proud of his gardens and of his superbly manicured croquet lawn. He discovered that Michael was a first-class croquet player, a member of the elite Westhampton Mallet Club, and challenged him to a match. It was long and fiercely contested. In the midst of it, David called to his wife, Herta, "You must come and watch. This is the best croquet player we have ever had at Touffou!" David won, and could scarcely conceal his delight. Could we stay on a second day? he wondered.

Back at our own vacation home, I wrote David a thank-you letter, telling him that each member of the Maas family had a pet memory of our stay at Touffou. Mine was the night in the keep, Michael's the architectural tour, and the girls loved changing into bathing suits in a "room" created by privet hedges.

D.O. wrote back: "*My* favorite memory of your visit was beating Michael at croquet."

David is a master of the verbal riposte. Dolores Zahn and I went to a luncheon where David was speaking. I introduced Dolores to David. "Oh," she said enthusiastically, "I'm so glad to meet you. I've been a David Ogilvy fan for years!"

David replied immediately, "So have I."

The late Jack Silverman, then head of Broadcast Operations, recalled a spirited exchange. He had supervised filming D.O. in a "fireside chat" that would be sent to all Ogilvy & Mather offices. David telexed Jack from London, asking to see the rough cut before the film was released.

Jack flew to London, met David at his office, and showed him the film. David approved it. He then told Jack he had his car outside, as he was on his way to the Royal Enclosure at Ascot, and offered to drop him at his hotel. Jack accepted. At that moment the film projectionist entered and handed Jack the film in his Louis Vuitton carrying case.

David was thunderstruck. "A Louis Vuitton carrying case? A Louis Vuitton carrying case! We must be paying you too much."

Without a blink, Jack Silverman replied, "David, how could I carry a film about *you* in anything less?"

Without a blink, David answered, "We are obviously paying you too little."

When all is said and done, what I remember best and respect most about David Ogilvy is his sensitivity to people, especially creative people.

Jay Schulberg, now creative head of Ogilvy & Mather, remembers that when he was promoted from junior to senior writer, he inherited a larger office with a sofa in it. It was only a plastic-covered job, but still a much coveted status symbol. One day David walked in, lay down on the sofa, and told Schulberg, "I think better when I lie down."

"If I did that, I'd probably get fired," Schulberg said. "And anyway, they're taking the sofa away."

"Why?" David asked.

"Because I'm not a vice president, so I don't rate a sofa."

"How stupid," David said. "Give me a piece of paper." He wrote. "Do not move this sofa. D.O."

Schulberg reports, "They never moved it."

Ron Hoff tells about this experience. "I had gotten upset, as creative people often do. I don't even remember what account it was, and I wrote David an emotional memo about the unfairness of it all. It was a really dreary memo. One of those memos that makes you feel good after you've written it, but not so good after you've *mailed* it. The very next day, my phone rang. It was David. He said: 'Ron, I just got your memo. I'll be right up.' His office was on the floor below and on the other side of the building. Within a minute, I saw him hurrying down the corridor to my office. He came in, sat down, and leaned forward. He had my memo in his hand. He said 'I want to do something about this. Let's decide *right now.*'

"I've never forgotten that responsiveness—that earnestness—that understanding," Hoff concludes. "He really knew what made us tick, didn't he?"

Judson Irish, for many years copy chief at Ogilvy & Mather, sums it up in a letter he wrote to David long after he left the agency: "I'm afraid I always took it for granted that you knew how stimulating and inspiring it was for me to work with you, especially back in those exciting early days when we were all young and eager and ambitious. You were a breath of fresh air on the advertising scene. You knew the sky was the limit, and you proved it. As I look at most advertising I see today, I wish you were back, in your red suspenders and shirtsleeves, pushing back the horizon and opening up challenging new vistas on every hand. I hope you're happy. *We all owe you a monumental debt.*"

Bless you, David.

Of Shoes and Ships and Flooring Wax, of Cabbages and Kings

I never worked on a shoe account at Ogilvy & Mather, but the Lewis Carroll reference was irresistible.

"'The time has come,' the Walrus said,/'To talk of many things:/ Of shoes—and ships—and sealing-wax—/ Of cabbages—and kings—'"

My typewriter at Ogilvy & Mather tapped away for a great ship, the *QE II,* Johnson Wax, Imperial Margarine with its "flavor fit for a king," and lots of other accounts. The cabbages, admittedly, are a reach. One summer, when the price of lettuce had skyrocketed, we tried to convince consumers to use Good Seasons salad dressing on cabbage. This attempt failed miserably.

My very first advertising assignment was to create a television commercial for a new dishwashing liquid, Dove-for-Dishes, a superb product made by Lever Brothers. Dove was so gentle that tests proved it could actually improve the appearance of a woman's hands while she washed the dishes!

People not in advertising often ask how copywriters and art directors "dream up" ideas for print advertisements and commercials. These ideas actually evolve from the strategy; a statement agreed upon (and sometimes bled over) by the client and the agency, as to whom the product should be sold, and why. The key items of a good strategy are: target audience, the benefit to the consumer, and the reason to believe that benefit, also known as a "support."

Our target audience for Dove Liquid was women with dry hands. The benefit: Dove would make hands soft and smooth. The support: a mixture of protective ingredients never before found in a dishwashing liquid.

Lay people, when they hear about strategies, almost always have another question. Doesn't this direction restrict creative freedom? Not any more than Shakespeare was fettered by the sonnet form or Beethoven by the structure of the symphony.

The year Dove-for-Dishes was launched was also the heyday of the "slice of life." My curiosity about this phrase led me to recall French literature. It is a direct translation of *tranche de vie,* a form of theater popular in the nineteenth century. It tried to imitate real life, but most of the plays are dreary or, at best, sweaty.

The "slice of life" works in advertising, because it is involving. At its best the slice shows you people who look and sound "real," talking about human problems to which the product provides a solution.

At their worst, these commercials are the inanities which have helped to make advertising a profession rated just below that of funeral-parlor director.

"Helen, why are you crying?"

"It's Joe, Alice. He's leaving me."

"Leaving you after ten years! Another woman?"

"Wax buildup."

That sort of commercial has given rise to the saying "Please don't tell my mother I'm in advertising. She thinks I play the piano in a whorehouse."

All television commercials are given informal titles, usually by the copywriter. Sometimes these names have come back to haunt me. I once received a grand award

before a glittering audience of my peers for a spot called
"Greasy Pan" for Drano. My first commercial for Dove
Liquid was "Cupcake." It opened with a mother in her
garden, doling out cupcakes to a brood of children, when
suddenly a dove flew past her and into the kitchen window of a neighbor's home. The character did a double
take, turned to the camera and exclaimed, "I could have
sworn I saw a *dove* fly into Susie Smith's kitchen!" She
then burst into her neighbor's kitchen and discovered the
dove, which turned magically into a bottle of the dishwashing liquid.

The mother expressed disbelief about a dishwashing
product that was actually good for hands. "With six kids
and my dry hands," I had her say, "I need a *miracle*." The
neighbor proudly displayed her own newly softened and
smoothed hands. The mother was won over. "This Dove-
for-Dishes *is* a miracle!"

I was drawing on much learned during my years on
"Name That Tune." A mother with lots of young children, a nurturing mother at that, a problem shared by
many viewers (dry hands) and a little Biblical language.
Roberta Semple Salter called me the moment she saw that
commercial on the air. "I knew it was you," she said. High
praise.

Before the commercial could be aired, however, it had
to be produced. The first step was casting. Casting departments of all too many agencies follow the advice of
Casablanca's Captain Renaud, "Round up the usual sus-
pects."

The casting crew at Ogilvy & Mather were tireless in
their pursuit of new talent. They discovered Mary Jo
Catlett, a plump young comedienne then playing the
soubrette in Broadway's *Hello, Dolly!* We cast her on the
spot as the mother.

All my years of television production had not prepared
me for the multitudes of people needed to film one

thirty-second television commercial. The agency people are there, as are representatives of the client. Their numbers vary according to the importance of the commercial, and where it is being filmed. Location shoots in California and/or the Caribbean are always Standing Room Only. Shelby Page, great comptroller of Ogilvy & Mather, devised Shelby's Law, "The number of people present at any filming increases in geometric proportion to the mean temperature of the location."

As a student of linguistics, I have always been fascinated by the language of the film studio. The union crew includes "grips" (because they grip things such as large pieces of furniture and transport them from one place to another?) and "gaffers" (because they used to carry long poles or gaffs in order to reach lights hung high overhead?). Portions of the commercial that do not require synchronized sound are filmed "MOS." This jargon is said to derive from the early days of the talkies, when a German director had finished with the dialogue and prepared to film bucolic scenery. "Ve vill shoot this *mitout* sound," he said, according to film buffs. Hence, MOS. Apocryphal? Probably.

The derivation of one film word has eluded me for years, and I will be grateful to William Safire, his Lexicographic Irregulars, or any reader who can solve the mystery. Filmmakers use a hunk of black cardboard, rather like a huge jigsaw piece, with holes cut in it at random, to create effects of light and shadow. It is called a "cookalouris." (The spelling is mine.) My best guess is that the word is a bastardized form of chiaroscuro. Correct answers are welcomed.

There is a damnable sword of Damocles suspended over the heads of most creative people who work on packaged goods. The Burke Test! It is research that assesses how many people who saw your commercial actually remember seeing it, or can recall anything about it.

Most major companies, such as Lever, General Foods, and Procter & Gamble, use a Burke test or its equivalent to decide whether a given commercial should run. If a commercial bores people or sends them off to the refrigerator, it will not sell the product. David Ogilvy always cautioned us, "You can't save souls in an empty church." The favorite children of most copywriters—commercials that are humorous, emotional, obscure, or far out—tend to fail in Burke testing. Clear presentation of a problem, with the product or service as solution, is a key to memorable advertising.

The "Cupcake" slice for Dove scored very well, and we were off and running. Dove-for-Dishes now had a campaign that could be "pooled out." Over the next three years I wrote a dozen more slices in the same vein. All of them featured a Doubting Thomas who became a true believer. Most of them relied on some of the old "Name That Tune" sure-fire emotional tugs: a newlywed; an "ugly duckling" transformed into a swan; a self-righteous husband who turned out to be wrong.

The National Organization for Women gave me their "Most Offensive Commercial of the Year" award for showing women at kitchen sinks. I reminded them that the very positioning of the product was for *women* with dry hands. However, my consciousness was raised sufficiently to add the character of a helpful husband who dried the dishes. He became a fixture of Dove Liquid advertising for years.

The National Organization for Women also led me, in a curious way, to the creation of a radio campaign for Dove Liquid that has a special place in my heart. It used men, faced with having to do dishes while their wives were away (having a baby, visiting mother), who suffered the embarrassment of noticeably soft, smooth hands.

In one radio spot, a tough construction worker remarked to his equally tough buddy, "Harry, your hands!

They're GORGEOUS. Elizabeth Taylor should only have your hands." Continuity clearance refused to accept the commercial, unless Miss Taylor gave her approval. I was young and feisty and approached her remarkable lawyer, Aaron Frosch, for permission. Happily for me, Frosch had a sense of humor, and okayed it. Gratefully, I sent him a case of Dove-for-Dishes.

My own husband was delighted about my new career and more helpful than any husband in any Dove commercial. The only bad days I recall were summer Saturdays, before we were making enough money to rent a summer home, much less own one. Michael would head off at dawn to play golf, and about 9 A.M. I would take Kate and Jenny to the Central Park playground, right across the street from our apartment on 95th Street. (We had progressed, since our marriage, from the tiny apartment on 91st Street to a slightly larger one on 93rd and then to a three-bedroom—imagine!—apartment on 95th Street just off Fifth Avenue.)

We went on the swings, and on the slide. We seesawed. We played in the sandbox. I vowed not to look at my watch just yet. We swung again, seesawed some more. It must be at least 11:00, I would muse. Almost time for lunch and naps. I would allow myself to sneak a look at the time: 9:25!

Gene Grayson gave me a nice raise because of the success of the Dove commercials, and Michael had risen to be a project manager of the firm he now runs, then known as Smith, Smith, Haines, Lundberg & Waehler. I also had an unexpected bonus. We did some research about women's reactions to the fragrance of Dove, and as an expert interviewer, I wandered around a supermarket with a microphone hidden under the lettuce in my cart, while a hidden camera filmed my conversations with women customers. The client liked the footage so much they asked that it be made into a commercial. There was no way to cut me out of it, so I ended up being featured in my own advertising. And Lever Brothers had to pay me residuals!

This bonanza, plus the higher salaries Michael and I were both making, made us rich enough to rent a house in Westhampton for the month of July. Being a city kid, I had never learned to drive. So, when Michael was at the Westhampton Country Club, and I needed to get to town, we'd simply stand in front of our house on Dune Road and hitchhike. The sight of me, with a five-year-old holding one hand and a baby in my arms, softened the hearts of even the most cynical. Mack trucks would come to a screeching halt. "Jesus, lady, don't you know how dangerous it is to hitchhike?" drivers thundered. "Get in." They would often drive miles out of their way to deliver me to supermarkets and pharmacies.

Because of "Name That Tune," television was a more familiar medium to me than print advertising of any kind. I always loved seeing my commercials on the air, of course, but nothing beat the day when I entered the subway at 86th Street and saw my poster for Dove. "My God," I cried, "there it is!" The entire car quieted for a moment, as subway cars do when any "crazy" is spotted.

The highest-scoring commercial I wrote for any client was for the Drackett Company's Liquid Drano. After the Crying Plumber had introduced the product, we moved to a second campaign, with yet another plumber, and that marvelous actor Jimmy Coco in the role. The commercial began with a housewife greeting the plumber. "Willie! Company's coming in two hours and I have a clogged drain!" Willie took out his jug of Liquid Drano and unclogged the drain before the eyes of the viewer. The Burke score told us that 66 percent of all the people who watched that commercial remembered it. Even more important, they could talk about why the product worked so well. (Jimmy Coco didn't hurt, either.)

Willie the Plumber joined the host of "continuing characters" created at Ogilvy & Mather. Creative Director Reva Korda said she once dreamed they all lived in the same village: Cora, the Yankee storekeeper for Maxwell House coffee (played by Margaret Hamilton, the Wicked Witch of the West, and a sweetheart in real life) on Main Street; Pete the Butcher for Shake 'n Bake across the way; the librarian for Ex-Lax up on the hill; "Grampa" for Country Time lemonade down in the hollow, and Titus Moody for Pepperidge Farm riding hither and yon in his horse-drawn cart.

Other agencies introduced similar characters: Mr. Whipple for Charmin; Madge the Manicurist for Palmolive dishwashing liquid; Rosie for Bounty paper towels. Lots of consumers say they dislike these characters and the often corny situations. But what they say and what they do are different matters. For many years Mr. Whipple headed the list of "most disliked" commercials. During those same years, Charmin was the country's leading toilet paper.

Many young creative people also look down their noses at the technique of the continuing character. Yet the use of a character identified with a product has many advantages: memorability that increases over time, a familiar setting and the possibility of dramatic or humorous situations. I never won any awards because of Willie the Plumber. But Ogilvy & Mather was awarded more assignments by the Drackett Company, and I became the second woman vice president at the agency.

Chairman Jock Elliott came to my office to congratulate me, but I wasn't there. I called him later that morning to confess I had stolen off for an hour to watch Kate appear in a class play at the Nightingale-Bamford School, but was planning to work through lunch to make up for it. "Go out and celebrate at lunch," Jock ordered. "At this agency, we encourage women to take time off to share important occasions with their children." He thought for a moment, and added, "I suspect we should begin urging *men* to do the same." Jock's mother, Audrey, had been one of the first and most fervent suffragettes. His talented wife, Elly, was an early member of Women's Forum and is director of the Legal Defense and Education Fund of the National Organization for Women. Jock has always been fiercely supportive of women, and was one of the driving forces behind their rise at Ogilvy & Mather.

Today, there are scads of women vice presidents and senior vice presidents at Ogilvy & Mather. My friend and fellow working mother Elaine Reiss is an executive vice president.

Seven years after I left Ogilvy & Mather, I volunteered to testify on the agency's behalf in a class action suit brought against them by a woman employee who claimed they discriminated against women. Bernice Kanner, in her advertising column in *New York* magazine, quoted me as saying that the suit was "barbarous" (I was borrowing a David Ogilvy word), since that agency had done more to advance women than any other.

In the witness box, I was grilled by the attorney for the plaintiff. She asked me when I had worked at Ogilvy & Mather. "From 1964 to 1976," I replied without hesitation.

She noted frostily that it was unusual, after all these years, for me to remember so precisely the year I began.

"Not really," I said, and held up my left arm. "I'm wearing my Ogilvy & Mather ten-year watch, and the date's inscribed right on it."

I had never been in a witness box before, and melted inside my suit as the questioning grew even sharper. I stuck to my guns and what I believe to be the truth: Women at Ogilvy & Mather are given opportunity and advancement equal to men. The judge found for Ogilvy & Mather. Justice prevailed.

The Drackett Company and its smart young president, Nick Evans, were joys to work with. Drackett is located in Cincinnati, near their giant competitor, Proctor & Gamble. Drackett was small and venturesome enough to turn on a dime. Once, when P & G's research indicated to them that adding lemon juice and lemon fragrance to almost any cleaning product would attract customers, the very air of Cincinnati smelled lemony. Drackett sniffed, then rushed new lemon-freshened products into the marketplace ahead of its rival.

Another of the joys of Drackett was working with account supervisor John Blaney, known to me as "Black Jack," one of the funniest—and most tender—men I have ever worked with.

As a young account executive, John, never a shrinking violet, went to the head of Ogilvy & Mather and asked to become a vice president.

"Why do you want to be a vice president, John?" Jim Heekin asked him. "*Everybody* is a vice president."

"Exactly," said John. He made his point, and has been getting promotions ever since. Well deserved.

When John's wife, Natalie, went back to get her law degree, John happily took over caring for their daughter, Megan, tended to household chores, and tripled the number of accounts he managed. He simply moves at a more efficient speed than most mortals.

I have long since forgiven him for letting his Saint Bernard, Churchill, eat our screen door in Westhampton.

While working for Drackett, I was also Queen of the Toilet Bowls. Their Vanish bathroom bowl cleaner was the leading product in its category. Vanish was another instance of strange things that happened before the women's liberation movement blossomed. The network clearance people, who ruled over the content and language of all commercials, declared it was fitting and proper to say "toilet bowl" during daytime hours, but allowed only "bathroom bowl" for nighttime viewing. Presumably, "toilet" was an offensive word to a man's ear.

Drackett created a new product: a *liquid* toilet-bowl cleaner. The commercial resulted in the discovery of Arte Johnson, long before he became one of the stars of television's "Laugh In." I went to California, where the spot was to be produced.

Michael asked me why on earth I had to go to California. Did they have better toilet bowls? The reason was a new film process called "humanization," by which the bottle of Vanish turned into a sort of lionlike creature that roared, and the production company that "humanized" was in Los Angeles. The premise of the commercial was that Liquid Vanish was "the angry bathroom bowl cleaner; it hates stains so much it wipes them out."

At the casting call, Arte Johnson was one of many actors who auditioned for the role. He was an unlikely spokesman. He had recently played the part of a concentration-camp survivor, and was more than normally emaciated and possessed of a scruffy beard. Under that mangy exterior was a great comic talent, perfect for a commercial intended to be funny. My group head, Gene Grayson, was due in two days to approve the casting. Would Arte try to gain five pounds and shave his beard? He blanched, but agreed. Gene Grayson approved wholeheartedly, and Arte indeed gave us a funny commercial.

The bottle that roared had to be superimposed separately during the film editing, so Arte had to *pretend* he was holding a bottle that huffed and puffed and carried on fiercely. No mean feat, but Arte achieved it. As the commercial progressed, the bottle grew progressively angrier, and Arte progressively more terrified. Watching the dailies, we knew we had a hit. Arte went on to loftier things.

Another talented young actor we discovered for Drackett was F. Murray Abraham. I cast him in one of the first commercials he ever made, for a now-defunct product called Whistle spray cleaner. He was called on to do a double take, and managed a *triple*.

"F. Murray," I said, taking him aside, "that's a really funny reaction. You're a wonderful actor."

"Am I really?" he asked earnestly. "Truly?" F. Murray displayed the same talent and humility almost twenty years later when he accepted the Academy Award for his performance in *Amadeus*.

At Ogilvy & Mather, creative people fought for the privilege of working on General Foods accounts. They demanded much of their copywriters and art directors, gave pointed and helpful criticism, and praised lavishly when praise was warranted.

More advertisers should realize that if they allow product managers to abuse the people who create their advertising, they will lose out in the end. The best creative people will ask for other assignments, and be replaced by drones or whipped dogs who can stomach this type of client.

Once, the creative head of another agency called to offer me a job writing for a notoriously difficult client. "Of course," he added quickly, "we keep writers on that account for only nine months. After that they have nervous breakdowns." I thanked him for his candor, but said I was perfectly happy at Ogilvy & Mather.

One Ogilvy client for whom I worked turned down thirty-three storyboards in succession. The account is no longer at the agency.

David Ogilvy, in his *Confessions,* tells of making a new business presentation to an association representing a number of different manufacturers. "Mr. Ogilvy," he was told, "we are interviewing several agencies. You have exactly fifteen minutes to plead your case. Then I will ring this bell, and the representative of the next agency, who is already waiting outside, will follow you."

David asked three questions, including how many of their many members would have to approve any given advertisement. Answer: all twelve members of the committee.

"Ring the bell," David said, and walked out.

This phrase became a watchword at the agency. When any of us were locked in struggle with intractable clients, one would whisper to the other, "Ring the bell!"

Sometimes, the shoe was on the other foot. Dave Braun, my client on Maxim Freeze-Dried Coffee, complained to account executive Dave Weiss that I was too accommodating, agreed too readily to his requests for copy changes. Weiss passed the information to me. At the very next creative presentation, Braun asked me to change the phrase "Maxim is sure good coffee" to "Maxim is sure a good coffee." I refused to add the "a." Braun pleaded. I remained adamant. "It's really a minor point," he offered.

"Exactly," I said coolly.

Braun later remarked to Weiss, "Jane Maas is one of the best copywriters I have ever worked with, but she sure can be stubborn." Dave Braun was one of the best clients I ever worked with. He now directs the entire media operation for all of General Foods,

Today I tell my creative people to report to me immediately if a client mistreats them. The worst form of mistreatment is to say, "I just don't like it. Come back with something else. I can't tell you exactly what I want, but I'll know it when I see it."

I have also always persuaded my creative troops that arrogance vis à vis clients is a sin. Too many copywriters, especially the young, present one layout or storyboard with a "take it or leave it" attitude. I prefer to present three ideas for any new advertising campaign. We always have a recommendation, but we listen hard to ideas from clients. Good clients often have very good ideas, because they know their product and its users.

I learned a lot about my craft while on General Foods. First, they gave us the most important ingredient in the success of any advertising campaign: a fine product. They believe in market research, and they respect the power of advertising.

Although most of my copywriting on General Foods was devoted to Maxim Coffee, I also wrote for several other food accounts. One was Start orange breakfast drink, where I worked with one of the first woman product managers at General Foods, Sandra Meyer. She went on to become president of the American Express Communications Company, then an Executive Director of Russell Reynolds associates. Another of my accounts was Open Pit barbecue sauce, for which I created a campaign that ran for more than ten years: testimonials by chefs of famous barbecue restaurants.

Some of the hardest work ever done by client and agency together is the development and positioning of new products. The best positioning always grows from the product or service. Mercedes-Benz was positioned not as the utmost in luxury, but as a superbly engineered car. Dove Beauty Bar, with its cleansing cream ingredient, was for women with dry skin.

Often, intensive market research is needed to be certain that the position is right. When General Foods created Shake 'n Bake, the agency and client felt that the best strategy was the promise of "a totally new taste in chicken." A number of focus group interviews, during which a moderator listened to potential customers react to the product and potential advertisements, convinced everyone that women didn't *want* a whole new taste in chicken. The strategy they responded to was "chicken that's crispy outside, moist and tender inside."

Heartened by the success of Shake 'n Bake, General

Foods developed a batter mix for chicken. The cook at home needed only to add milk and egg, dip the chicken in the batter, and deep-fry it. The result was Kentucky Fried Chicken gone to heaven. We named it Batter Fry, and created advertising loaded with appetite appeal. The positioning was "old-fashioned batter-fried chicken you can make *easily.*"

All the research looked positive. Consumers liked the concept. Adults liked the taste of the product; children adored it. Kate and Jenny certainly did the first and only time I took the product home and tried it myself. I swore I would never make it again. The kitchen filled with the greasy fumes of deep frying. My own experience should have given me a clue. After a short while in test market, Batter Fry was clearly a mistake. It was another lesson in how to read research: Pay attention to what consumers do, not what they tell you they are going to do. Women who were potential purchasers of the product said they loved the taste. They did not admit one important fact of life; they loathed the mess and bother of deep frying.

It was one of General Foods's rare failures. However, as the authors of *In Search of Excellence* tell us, excellent companies look for a certain number of failures every year. It is the only way management can be sure enough risks have been taken. Remember the words of Robert Browning: "Ah, but a man's reach should exceed his grasp,/ Or what's a Heaven for?"

There was one new product assignment from General Foods that I felt sure was doomed to fail. It was so top secret that we were asked to refer to it only with its code name: Project Acorn. ("Tall oaks from little acorns grow.") I figured this product was going to be not an oak, but a disaster. During a period when coffee prices were rising steeply, and consumers drinking less of it, General Foods determined to produce a coffee whose whole *raison d'être* was its low price. The product was to be a mixture of coffee, other less-expensive ingredients such as chicory, and a little molasses to kill the bitter taste of the chicory.

I entered the first focus group session armed with concepts that were basically different ways of saying: cheap coffee! The women in the groups revolted. One said, "I'd stop serving meat before I'd compromise on coffee." The others agreed with her. When they tasted the prototypical new coffee, they hated it.

The young product manager from General Foods looked at me with the wide, sad eyes of a calf. He saw his promising career coming to a premature end. "Hang in," I said. We had a one-hour break before the next group of women were expected. I tore up the original concepts, borrowed a desk and typewriter from the secretary of the research organization, and started to write concepts from scratch. One was "New coffee made the old-fashioned American way." (I had read that pioneers, crossing the prairie, brewed coffee from exactly these ingredients.) Another concept was "Now, the great taste of Scandinavian coffees comes to America!" (More research had indicated that the coffees of Scandinavia often owed their rich taste to the same kind of brew.) And the third was "Now, rich coffee without the bitter taste!" This concept explained that the molasses smoothed out the taste of the chicory.

The product manager looked at Concept #3 and choked. "Are you really going to show that to them?" I said we might as well find out the worst.

The group of twelve women filed in and took their seats behind the one-way mirror. They thought coffee made the old American way was fine. They were intrigued by coffee made the Scandinavian way. But coffee made with chicory and molasses that would taste rich and never bitter was dynamite! When they tasted the test product, exactly the same coffee sampled by the previous group, they pronounced it delicious.

The product manager looked like a condemned man receiving a reprieve. Project Acorn grew into an oak indeed: In other creative hands at a different agency it became a product called Master Blend.

General Foods often asked its agencies to present informative seminars. Ken Roman (then a young vice president and account supervisor on several General Foods products, now president of Ogilvy & Mather) had an idea. He suggested that we work as a team, account person and creative person, in putting together a seminar to teach clients how to look at rough layouts and storyboards and know whether they will turn into successful advertisements and commercials. Our seminar was a hit with the Maxwell House division, and Roman and Maas became a popular road show.

Ken had another idea. "I think we have a book on our hands," he said. I agreed to be his co-author. We were too dumb to get ourselves an agent at the outset, or to find an interested publisher. We just sat down and wrote the whole thing. It took us two years.

How do two people write a book together? I don't know how Beaumont and Fletcher worked, but Ken and I found it easy. He'd write chapter one, I'd write chapter two, then we'd switch, read and revise each other's work, switch again, revise again. We cannot read the book today and recognize which one of us wrote a given sentence. True collaboration.

After two years and several rewrites, we asked Andrew Kershaw, president of Ogilvy & Mather, to read the manuscript. He responded in twenty-four hours. "Once more unto the breach, dear friends, once more." We returned to our typewriters.

One year later, Andrew deemed the manuscript good

enough to send along to David Ogilvy. We asked for con-
structive criticism. David returned the pages in less than
one week. Not a single paragraph was untouched by his
red pen. *Every* paragraph was improved. David Ogilvy is
the best editor in the business.

"I hope I have not butchered your baby," he wrote us,
and confessed he was like his friend Marvin Bower. "It is
said of him that if you send him an engraved wedding
invitation, he will send it back to you, edited."

David said, further, that he did not care for any of the
more than one hundred titles we had submitted to him.
"I will give you the title I was planning to use for *my* next
book."

The manuscript was submitted to eighteen publishers
by our patient and cheerful agent, Julian Bach. Seven-
teen of them said no; the eighteenth, St. Martin's Press,
agreed to publish it. Our editor said that one title was
clearly better than any of the others. It was David
Ogilvy's, of course. Today, *How to Advertise* is the second
most popular book on advertising ever written. What
book is first? David Ogilvy's *Confessions of an Advertising
Man.* No surprise.

Our book has been published in German, Italian, English (with spellings changed for proper UK usage),
Spanish, Chinese, and Japanese. When I made a speech
in Tokyo, I was invited to visit Dentsu, the largest advertising agency in the world, and granted an interview with
its legendary managing director, Hideharu Tamaru.

With the help of an interpreter, we had a spirited conversation about advertising. He motioned to the Japanese
edition of *How to Advertise* which lay on his table, and
asked about the opening paragraph. Ken and I state that
advertising has borrowed the language of war. We discuss
strategies, we wage campaigns, we aim advertising messages at targets.

"I have always thought this true," Mr. Tamaru said

gravely, "but you are the first to express it. We have had enough of war. Our industry should find other words." I agree.

My friend Jane Trahey, in her book *Women and Power,* says that all the successful women she interviewed during her research had the support of a powerful mentor. Gene Grayson was one mentor of mine. Another was Andrew Kershaw. During his regime, the agency promoted me to the position of "syndicate head." That title may smack of Mafiadom to you. David Ogilvy so named his creative chiefs, because the word conjured up the era of merchant barons whose syndicates made it possible for the Drakes and Raleighs to explore new worlds. We syndicate heads knew what grail we sought: new worlds in advertising.

In my syndicate were fourteen people: copywriters, art directors, producers and secretaries. The products we advertised ranged from Dove Beauty Bar to the Bowery Savings Bank, with spokesman Joe DiMaggio. The cleansing cream pouring into the bar of Dove had been working more than twenty years. DiMaggio had been increasing deposits at the Bowery for more than two. I had the good sense not to fiddle with either of them.

Among the products in my group was Old Crow bourbon. The building that housed National Distillers, its maker, shuddered as I entered. I was the first woman ever to work on the brand. Liquor was then very much a man's world. The first advertisement that showed a woman even *holding* a drink in her hand was considered daring.

The Johnson Wax Company was looking for an agency to add to its roster, and Andrew Kershaw asked me to be part of the new business presentation. He had me flown to New York in a seaplane from Barnegat, New Jersey, where Michael and I were visiting my surrogate parents, Mary and Ken Leiby.

Michael and I stood on the beach as the plane roared

in and landed about fifty feet from the shore. I waited for some ramp to materialize. Michael laughed. "He's not going to get any closer," said my ex-Marine knowingly. I removed my shoes and pantyhose, wrapped the skirt of my silk suit around my thighs, and waded out to the plane. I was still damp when we made the pitch.

New business presentations sometimes go wonderfully well. And sometimes they don't. Charlie Fredericks and I once visited a remote Caribbean island to make a pitch for their tourism business. We flew to Miami, changed to a smaller plane, and flew to a large island. There, we were told to board an even smaller plane, bound for the smaller island, and warned that weight allowances would not permit us to take along the film projector we were carrying with us.

The film projector at the Ministry of Tourism chewed up our film and spit it out in the middle of the presentation, so we turned to our slides. "Now," Charlie said, "I want to show you what we have done for our client, TWA." He pressed the button, and there was the photo of a TWA 747, upside down.

I flew out to Vail, Colorado, with a client from American Express, to help make a presentation to the Rocky Mountain Ski Association on behalf of the American Express Card. We were to present to the group an advertisement which I had written. "Don't let on that you don't know how to ski," my client warned. "You might lose credibility."

The Ski Association people were gracious hosts. They regretted it was May, so I would have no chance to ski, but offered me a gondola ride. I accepted. We arrived at the top of the mountain, where I realized they were proposing to hurl me across a chasm in a car attached to a wire. "Oh my God," I screamed. Perhaps they suspected I had never been on skis.

We did win the Johnson Wax business, including Favor

furniture polish and Glade air fresheners. During our first visit to headquarters in Racine, Wisconsin, Mr. Sam Johnson, son of the founder, greeted his entire new agency team at a dinner party. "My products have to be top quality," he told us. "My name is on every one."

We were fascinated by the headquarters building, which had been designed by Frank Lloyd Wright. On our second visit, we discovered it leaked like a sieve in heavy rain. The secretaries ran around with buckets.

Life wasn't easy for secretaries at Johnson Wax. The company clung to the three-legged secretarial chairs also designed by Wright. If the occupant does not keep both feet firmly planted on the floor, the chair throws her head over heels. Perhaps Wright wanted to maintain proper secretarial decorum. (The chairs reminded me of the old Bucknell "Three feet on the floor" rule, designed to protect the virtue of coeds. When we entertained gentlemen in Hunt Hall living room on a Saturday night, out of any four respective feet, three had to be on the floor. Housemothers checked.)

Our syndicate came up with at least one significant bit of marketing for the Johnson Wax company. We gave them the positioning for their new Glade Solid air freshener. "It works like an air conditioner." My friend Jay Schulberg took that concept and made a witty and successful introductory commercial for Glade.

The members of our syndicate were good friends. We did lots of things together. One day, a group of us decided to quit smoking. Somebody knew a man who specialized in helping people quit, and we all chipped in to have him coach us. After two weeks, we were instructed to throw away our cigarettes at midnight. The next day I made the rounds to see how my troops were doing. Copywriter Marianne Baer was at her desk, sobbing. "I will never be able to write again." I moved on to the next office, where an art director, who shall be nameless, was wildly drunk. "I don't mish it," he confided. Was anyone alive and working? I heard the sound of typing from Peter Hochstein's office. There he was, working furiously. Thank goodness, I thought, Peter's okay. Peter turned to see who had entered his office. He was fiercely sucking a pacifier.

The syndicate went back to smoking. A few years later, I went to Smoke Enders. They promised me I would quit without pain or sense of loss, and never want a cigarette again. They made good their promise.

One of the perks of becoming a syndicate head was gaining membership to the executive dining room, known as "Rose's Room," after Rose, the cook who presided. There was good food, an open bar, good wine, and all manner of soft drinks. I don't usually drink at lunch, so I toasted my first official visit to Rose's Room in Perrier. "Have a Scotch," Andrew Kershaw urged. "It's cheaper."

David Ogilvy insisted that we bring no documents to Rose's Room. He forced one culprit to stuff his papers back into an attaché case and end a business conversation. "You wouldn't carry on like that at a good club," D.O. chided.

During one of my first luncheons at Rose's Room, I was seated next to a client, whose name, title, and corporate connection went unheard in the babble of conversation. "I understand that you and Ken Roman are about to publish a book," he commented. "And there's a chapter on how to be a better client."

I mumbled agreement.

"Who's your favorite client? The one you most enjoy working with?" All conversation stopped. The eyes and ears of Rose's Room turned to me. I took a deep breath. "There are lots of clients I like, but the one who is most consistent in getting good work from the agency is General Foods."

My unknown companion asked why.

"Because the people we work with are ladies and gentlemen, never bullies. So creative people *like* working with them."

"I'm going to remember that advice," he said, and shook my hand. Later, Bill Phillips told me I would be allowed back into Rose's Room anytime. The mystery client was Jim Ferguson, then head of the Birds Eye Division of General Foods. He is now chairman and chief executive of the company. And a gentleman with brains.

Another pleasant result of my new title was a raise. Michael became a junior partner of his firm, and we bought a little red house in Westhampton. Kate and Jenny were fascinated. It had *stairs*! As city children, they had never lived in a home with an upstairs and a downstairs.

The house had lots of land, so I, a child of the city, took to gardening. I was like a virgin discovering sex. Nobody told me that twenty tomato plants would yield enough tomatoes to feed the world. My mother visited and helped me can some of the crop, but friends and colleagues ran from me, my tomatoes, and my mason jars. The next year, we gave up the garden and put in a swimming pool.

My last several years at Ogilvy & Mather were the most fun because of two people, one real, one imaginary: Academy Award winner Patricia Neal, and Josiah S. Carberry, the world's most traveled man.

Patricia Neal became the spokesman for Maxim Coffee in 1972. The campaign, because of Pat herself, was brilliant, and ran for almost four years. The consequences for Pat's personal life were totally unexpected.

Maxim, the world's first freeze-dried coffee, was looking for the right strategy to combat its successful archenemy, Taster's Choice. Maxim had been launched some years earlier, on a "tastes like fresh-perked" strategy. One year later, Taster's Choice appeared on the market, following exactly the same strategy.

Now General Foods wanted to find another niche, a positioning that would set us apart from our competition. All of us at the agency and the client knew from our mountains of research that the best strategy for any coffee in a jar is a promise of fresh-perked flavor. Another important element showed up in the research. Men! Men had strong "negative veto" over coffee purchase. If a man drank his coffee and said nothing, that was praise enough. If, however, a husband commended his wife on her coffee and asked for a *second* cup, she would be loyal to that coffee forever. Let him complain or refuse seconds, and she would shop for a different brand.

At Ogilvy & Mather, we decided that we needed a memorable, persuasive commercial that would score high on the Burke test. We agreed on a celebrity testimonial. And who would be a more credible choice, given a husband-pleasing strategy, than Patricia Neal?

Only a few years earlier, Pat had suffered a massive stroke, and doctors predicted she would never regain her speech. Most people know the story of how her husband, English writer Roald Dahl, refused to accept this verdict. He goaded Pat, cajoled her, urged her onward. He marshaled an army of their neighbors to give Pat virtually round-the-clock therapy. Patricia Neal recovered completely and returned to stardom. Pat said often and publicly that she owed it all to Roald Dahl. A two-hour made-for-television movie, called *The Patricia Neal Story*, stars Glenda Jackson as Pat, Dirk Bogarde as Roald, and purports to tell the entire experience. My friendship with Pat let me in on the truth: the *real* Patricia Neal story.

As soon as General Foods agreed that Patricia Neal was our first choice, I telephoned the Dahl home in Great Missenden, England. The housekeeper answered and I explained my mission. There was a pause, then Pat was on the telephone. "I'm Jane Maas," I began.

"Hello, Jane Maas," Pat replied, in that husky voice that is her trademark. We have been friends ever since that moment.

Pat and Roald had enjoyed Maxim in the United States, but could not find it in England. Legal regulations for a celebrity endorsement dictated that both Pat and Roald had to drink the coffee for at least several months before a commercial could be filmed. (This rule went into effect shortly after a well-known actor, then appearing in commercials on behalf of a shaving cream, was asked by a talk show host if he really liked the stuff. "I dunno," the actor said. "Never used it.")

After two months, things looked good enough for us to begin contract negotiations with Roald, who acted as Pat's business manager. He asked for and received a good fee for Pat's endorsement for one year. If commercials were filmed in the United States, Pat would be given two first-class round-trip tickets, in case she wanted to bring along a companion. A reasonable demand. There was another Dahl fiat that gave me pause. He demanded script approval.

We decided to film the first two commercials in London, feeling it might be easier for Pat to be near home. I wrote two thirty-second commercials, one called "Morning Maxim," the other "Evening Maxim." The first was to open on Pat at breakfast. On the table were hot buttered muffins (research said coffee was more appetizing when shown with other food) and a jar of Maxim. Pat's opening line was, "My husband loves a good breakfast. And good coffee. That's why I serve him Maxim." Pat would then make two cups of Maxim, sip one with pleasure and conclude, "My husband says Maxim tastes like fresh-perked coffee. And I never argue with him. Especially when he's right."

The second commercial was an after-dinner scene, with Pat declaring, "I love this hour. Children in bed, alone with my husband. And a good cup of coffee. Maxim." Both commercials were to be filmed as though Roald Dahl were to enter the scene any moment.

The scripts were approved by General Foods and, after some squabbling over words, by Roald. We agreed on an American director and a London film production company. The agency art director, Mark Ross (now a film director in his own right), and the director, Norman Griner, flew over three days before filming to approve the sets, props and wardrobe.

I left for London two days before the shooting. The hem of my coat was sagging, I noticed as I boarded the plane, so I whipped out my traveling sewing kit and stitched away. My seatmate, a distinguished-looking Englishman, turned to me well into this performance. "Are you a seamstress?" he asked.

"No," I told him. "I'm in advertising. What do you do?"

"Actually," he said, "I'm Lord Mayor of London." We flew on in silence.

Next morning, after one of those sleepless, jet-lagged nights, a car and driver came to take me to Great Missenden for a script rehearsal with Pat.

We arrived at Gypsy House, the Dahls' sixteenth-century manor in the countryside near Great Missenden. It was a warm day in early June. When Pat came out to say hello, I thought that she looked even more beautiful than in her films.

It was hard not to be in awe of Pat. She had been a star ever since she made her screen debut, opposite Ronald Reagan, in *John Loves Mary*. She was one of the most beautiful women in films when, at the age of twenty-two, she made *The Fountainhead* with Gary Cooper. Pat starred in dozens of films, including my own favorite, *In Harm's Way*, opposite John Wayne; *The Hasty Heart; A Face in the Crowd.*

Her greatest role was that of the housekeeper in *Hud*, opposite Paul Newman, for which Pat won the Academy Award as best actress. And there she stood, in her doorway at Great Missenden, framed by roses as big as cabbages, about to rehearse words I had written.

Roald appeared, and insisted I take a tour of Gypsy House and its environs. Pat is tall, about five feet eight; Roald towered above her. He's a rugged man, at once very sexy and very paternal. It was easy to see why Pat, who had her choice of Hollywood's most eligible bachelors, had fallen for him.

The housekeeper prepared a simple lunch, served with wine, followed by fruit and Maxim. Roald explained that none of the children was at home. Their son Theo was away at boarding school. Their daughters, Tessa, Ophelia, and Lucy, were at local schools and might turn up before I left for London.

Roald fumed about "all the fuss and feathers" attendant upon making a commercial. "One would think we were making a feature film. The art director and that other chap, the one with the beard, the director, were here yesterday in a great bloody limousine as long as the *Queen Mary*." Only one part of the production process pleased him. The sets, props, and costumes were all handled by a firm established by two young Englishwomen of distinguished background. One of them, Felicity Crossland, had been obliging enough to make three trips to Great Missenden, offering up different selections for Pat to wear in the commercials, until Roald was satisfied.

After lunch, we got to the business at hand: rehearsal. Pat had received the final scripts several weeks before, and said she was comfortable with them. I took out my stopwatch, and signaled Pat to start reading. It was immediately obvious that she was going to be fabulous.

Pat and I rode into London. Roald was to join us that evening for dinner. I admired her mink jacket. She patted it affectionately. "Gary Cooper gave it to me. I was in love with him for a long time," she added candidly. "But he was married, and believed in marriage, so there was no hope. Oh, he was a beautiful man." She talked about meeting Roald at a dinner party, about their marriage, about the illness and death of their first child, Olivia.

We stopped at the pretty old village of Little Missenden to visit the eleventh-century church where Olivia is buried. Pat pointed out the Anglo-Saxon inscription carved into the stone of the even earlier foundation, by a grateful soldier returning home from some distant war. "There's always something to be happy about," Pat reflected. She left a few of Roald's big roses on Olivia's grave, and we drove on to London.

That night, six of us met for dinner at Roald's posh London club. In addition to the Dahls, we were joined by Dave Weiss, director Norman Griner, and art director Mark Ross, who had borrowed jacket and tie from Griner for the occasion, since he'd brought none to London.

Roald ordered for all of us. Prawns were the first course. I started in on mine. "No, no, no," Roald chided. "My God, why is it Americans know nothing about eating prawns!" After dinner, Roald invited the party to join him upstairs at the club's gambling casino. I had one foot on the stair when Roald stopped me. He packed Pat and me off to the hotel, under orders to go right to bed. There was no room for argument.

Next morning at seven we arrived at the London house that was serving as our location. The day was gloomy, but the breakfast room was lighted so that sun seemed to stream through the window. Pat, already in her costume, was in curlers, having makeup. I congratulated Felicity, a pert young woman, on the choice of clothing for Pat. The morning outfit was a soft, flattering blouse and simple skirt; the evening choice a long hostess gown. Young Felicity told me she'd made three separate trips to Great Missenden in the past few days before Mr. Dahl approved her choices. I mentioned that he had commented on her eagerness to please.

"Oh," Felicity said, "I would have made *ten* trips!"

It was time for the filming to begin. Pat, looking radiant, sat at the breakfast table. The prop man delivered the hot muffins, with the butter just beginning to melt. The director called "Action." Nothing happened. Then someone realized this was England. The direction for camera and sound to start recording is not "Action" but "Turn it over."

The prop man delivered a second plate of hot muffins. The director called "Turn it over!" We were off and running. By midafternoon, "Morning Maxim" was "in the can." While the crew set up for the next commercial, Pat had a cup of coffee and I called Roald, back home in Great Missenden, to tell him that things were going splendidly. Felicity, supervising the pressing of the hostess gown, listened as I spoke with Roald. "Do tell him Pat looks just beautiful," she said. I delivered the message.

"I was sure she would," Roald said.

We finished "Evening Maxim" just at dark. Pat had completed two demanding commercials in one day! The crew gave her a standing ovation.

Back in New York, we edited both commercials and put them on the air. The results of the Burke Recall Test suggested it was going to be a persuasive and successful campaign for Maxim. That's exactly what it was.

The next few years saw us filming about four commercials yearly, always, for some reason, in New York. We tried different situations. One spot had Pat in period costume, purportedly acting in a television special, shown taking a break as a stagehand brought her a cup of Maxim.

For another commercial, we wrote in a part for Pat and Roald's fifteen-year-old daughter, Tessa. I'd never met Tessa, but felt that the addition of another family member would add human interest to the commercial. Pat was already in New York for the filming, having come from Hollywood. We sent our young account executive out to the airport to meet Tessa. We had a photograph of her, a close-up of her face, and told John to look for a pretty teenager with long dark hair. John, a short, slim man, spent an hour in the baggage claim area, seeking vainly for Tessa. It finally dawned on him that the sophisticated, almost six-foot beauty who waited there was "our little Tessa."

We showed Pat in her kitchen, watering plants, making coffee. We showed her shopping. We tried a kind of candid-camera technique, in which I stood out of range of camera and asked Pat questions she wasn't prepared for in advance. One such question was, "Tell us about your husband. Is he a demanding man?"

Pat threw back her head and laughed. "My husband is a very demanding man. Demanding about everything." She glanced at me and remembered she was making a Maxim commercial. "Especially his coffee."

Roald and I battled over many of the scripts. In one situation, I had Pat talking about "company coming for dinner." Roald scoffed at me over the telephone. "Company is such a middle-class word," he said. "It's so *American.*"

"So are the people drinking the coffee," I shot back.

Pat's highest-scoring commercial was for a new, improved product. We showed Pat standing in "her" kitchen, a special set that was carefully stored away between commercials, and reconstructed so the clock hung in exactly the same place, the copper pots in the same order on the wall. Pat looked straight at the camera and confided, "I've found a coffee my husband likes even better than Maxim. It's *new* Maxim."

An old device, but an effective one. The commercial scored a whopping 34, 16 points over the Burke norm. My dear friend and client Dave Braun called to tell me the score, and I cried with relief. That night I threw a party at our home for everybody in the syndicate. We all wore handmade buttons saying "34!" No other creative group at Ogilvy & Mather that year had done so well for the Maxwell House Division.

It was fun working with Pat professionally. It was a joy becoming her friend. Pat adored my husband at first sight, and told him he reminded her of the architect hero of *The Fountainhead*. One evening, Pat, Michael, and I were coming down in the elevator of the St. Regis Hotel, where Pat liked to stay. "Tell me," Michael asked. "What's the real difference between Gary Cooper and me?"

Pat, who stood about three inches higher than Michael in her heels, glanced down at him affectionately. "Coop was taller."

Wherever we went to dinner in New York City, from "21" to Lutèce, I arranged that Maxim be served after dinner. Not one restaurant gave us any argument. Patricia Neal's name was magic. People fell over themselves to do anything she wanted.

The Neal campaign for Maxim, after a long and successful run, finally suffered what is known as "wearout." General Foods, those dear and generous clients, threw a big farewell party for Pat. They asked Sue Conrad, then account supervisor, and me what would be an appropriate gift. Sue and I knew that the Gary Cooper mink jacket had come to the end of its road, and suggested a replacement. General Foods agreed. The last time I saw Pat, she was wearing it; she calls it "my Maxim mink."

Pat and I remained friends after the Maxim campaign

ended, and are friends now. In 1982, almost ten years to the day after our first meeting in Great Missenden, Pat called me. She was in New York. Would I come and see her? I rushed to meet her.

Pat asked me if I remembered that first commercial we filmed in London. How could I forget it? And did I remember the young woman who had made all those trips to the Dahl home until Roald declared the clothes perfect? I did indeed.

"Well," Pat said, "Roald has just told me he is getting a divorce. He is going to marry Felicity and just think, my darling, *you* introduced them."

Pat told me that Roald and Felicity had been seeing each other for these past ten years. I wondered if any other television commercial has been responsible for so dramatically changing the course of someone's life.

After the Neal campaign ended, I felt I needed another window on the world. Andrew Kershaw waved his wand, and I was assigned to the American Express account, especially to the Travel Services Division.

The agency was busily creating charming and effective advertising for American Express, all under the new "Don't leave home without it" slogan. Karl Malden had just become spokesman for American Express Travelers Cheques. Creative director Bill Taylor and his merry band were filming the first commercials in the "Do You Know Me?" campaign, which is still running. Among the first of the "unknown faces" featured was Bill Miller, unsuccessful Vice Presidential candidate.

I worked briefly on The Card and on Space Bank, a hotel reservation service, now defunct. George Waters, one of the most senior officers at American Express, was in charge of Space Bank. I was warned that his temper was often short, and, since he was not accustomed to working with women, I was to wear my most tailored suit for our first meeting and under no circumstances to cry.

George Waters greeted the group from the agency pleasantly enough and was especially courteous to me. What a charming man, I thought. Why all the fuss? Then Waters handed me a pencil and a steno pad. He assumed I was a secretary, come to take notes on the meeting. To his credit, he recovered gracefully, and we had a terrific relationship as long as Space Bank lasted.

The Travel Division didn't have nearly as big a war chest to spend on advertising as did its sister divisions. Suzan Couch, newly appointed vice president, director of Advertising and Sales Promotion, had an inspired solution. Her background included heading up advertising for Macy's and sales and marketing jobs at several New York radio stations. She knew the power of radio to move people into stores, whether they were department stores or American Express Travel offices. We decided to do a radio campaign.

I remembered reading about a mythical figure created at Brown University in the 1920s—Josiah S. Carberry, the world's most traveled man. Who would know more about travel? Josiah was officially professor of psychoceramics at Brown. One year, he managed to circumnavigate the globe in twenty-four hours. Postcards mailed to Brown, simultaneously postmarked everywhere from Hong Kong to London, are proof of the feat.

The first Carberry radio script had him interviewed on a talk show. "I know you are the world's most traveled man, Mr. Carberry," the host said. "So we are very pleased to have you here."

"Yes," Carberry replied. "I am so seldom *here,* you know. Mostly I'm *there.*" He added that only yesterday he had returned from the Himalayas, where he'd been attending the games, of course.

Suzan Couch, good client that she is, took one look at the script, whooped with glee, and we were off. We chose to produce the commercials in California, to use the comic directing and performing talents of Alan Barzman, with whom Suzan had worked before. As Josiah, we cast Pat Harrington, Jr., and "Barz" helped us round up the talents of a unique group of California actors known unofficially as "voice people." They specialize in improvisation and are a breed apart.

It has often been said that if you sent to Central Casting for the perfect executive blonde, they would send you Suzan Couch. She is very tall, very slim, and very tan all year round. During the winter she wears a fox coat of outrageous proportions; duri..g the summer, equally outrageous bikinis. I have never known her to go into any body of water except her own hot tub.

During our first trip to California, we made the first of many stays at the Beverly Hills Hotel. It is still one of the great hotels of the world. Within moments after you check in, pick up the telephone and the operator greets you with "Yes, Mrs. Maas." Properly pronounced, too. We had one free evening the night before the recording session, and I alerted architect Jim Luckman, an old friend of Michael's and mine, that I'd be in his home town. Jim immediately invited me to dinner. "I have a client along," I said.

"Can't you ditch the client?" Jim asked. I told him there was no way.

"Oh, hell," Jim said. "Then bring him."

When I showed up with Suzan in tow—or the other way around—Luckman, then a bachelor, was bemused. "Things are looking up on the client front," he said. "How come I don't have any who look like that?" I warned him that Suzan was married, and we had a lovely, if decorous evening.

Commercials took Carberry from Acapulco Bay to the Black Forest, from Scotland to Rio, a city that prompted one spirited interchange.

MAN: Welcome to Rio, Mr. Carberry. Have you tried feijoada?
CARBERRY: Why, no. I'm afraid I've been too busy with Frieda.
MAN: Mr. Carberry, feijoada is a famous Brazilian dish.
CARBERRY: You should see Frieda.

In every commercial, Josiah's travel arrangements were made by American Express. He would not have it any other way. I wrote script after script for my famous traveler, taking him to locations that would have cost a fortune to translate to television. Radio has the unique ability to stretch the imagination of the listener. Stan Freberg once wrote a wonderful commercial on behalf of the Radio Advertising Bureau to demonstrate that power. He drained Lake Erie, filled it full of whipped cream, and had the Royal Air Force fly over to drop a maraschino cherry. Try doing that in a television commercial!

Josiah was a great success for American Express. From the very first day that his commercials ran in New York, business in local Travel Service offices doubled. Disk jockeys and radio talk-show hosts joked about Josiah, adding precious minutes of free commercial airtime.

Since Josiah was not truly a creation of mine, I had early on consulted the head of legal services at the agency, Elaine Reiss. Elaine said there was no need to get permission from Brown University to use Josiah, since he was a myth. Nobody, she explained, could own a myth.

Alas, it was not that simple. Charles Tillinghast, alumnus of Brown and chairman of the board of TWA, complained to his good friends at American Express that they were exploiting a beloved academic symbol for commercial gain. Josiah vanished from the airwaves.

Gone, but not forgotten by many of us. When Aldo Papone, president of the American Express Travel Division, left for another position, I had Josiah send him a telegram. "Congratulations and good luck. I will be watching you from afar. Or possibly from Anear, where I will be spending the summer."

A few years later, when Aldo returned to American Express as its vice chairman, Josiah (and I) sent him a second message: "Welcome 1 ome and congratulations, from the world's *second* most traveled man, Josiah S. Carberry."

Suzan Couch, no longer a client, remains a friend. Always an entrepreneur at heart, she has become a marketing consultant, with blue-chip clients in the fields of communication, especially television. We have an annual Josiah luncheon at "21" and reminisce.

One of our more frantic post-Josiah experiences was the filming of the first television commercial for Travel Service, in Venice. We imported an American actor, hired an Italian director and a Yugoslavian crew, and filmed all day in St. Mark's Square. Whatever *could* go wrong, did.

Even the pigeons deserted us. We had fed them so much corn the previous day during rehearsals, that, sated, they took the day off. The Italian director shouted "Action," which was translated into Yugoslavian by the script girl, then back into English as a signal for our actor-spokesman to walk across the square toward the camera.

Suzan Couch hated the way he walked. "He looks so jerky," she complained. "Like somebody on strings." The more Suzan spoke to him about striding confidently across the square, the more the actor jerked. He was terrified of her.

We flew to Rome to look at dailies. There was our actor, jiggling out of control across St. Mark's square like a Charlie Chaplin doll. "God," Suzan whispered to me, "he's even worse than I thought." Only when the director screamed did we realize the worst nightmare of film production had happened to us. Inadvertently, the camera had been undercranked, so all the footage was speeded up like an old silent movie.

We raced back to New York with our wounded footage, and worked for two days and nights without sleep to make the deadline for integration into the network feed for the Tony show. The editor was Chinese, and the script girl's cues and comments were all in Yugoslavian, so things went slowly.

The final step, after slowing the film down to normal with some electronic process, was having the actor re-read his lines to synchronize with the new speed of his mouth. We were in the control room; the actor was in a booth with earphones, watching the film, trying to match his own lip movements.

We tried take after take. He wasn't even close. Suzan fumed. More takes. Suzan got up and went into the booth. I watched as our distraught actor, more terrified of Suzan than ever, burst into tears.

The agency producer, who had lived through the whole experience, starting with the pigeons, sat beside me. "Who do you have to screw to get off this shoot?" he asked."

Ogilvy & Mather was my cherished home for twelve years. During that time, my salary quadrupled, and I rose from copy cub to a position as one of the creative directors. Only one force could entice me away, and it beckoned.

Wells, Rich, Greene called and asked me to come and work on Procter & Gamble. During all our years of writing *How to Advertise*, Ken Roman and I had speculated about what P & G knew that the rest of us did not. After agonizing over the choice, I accepted the offer.

Ogilvy & Mather threw me a princely farewell party, for which I was asked to draw up the guest list. It included Chairman Jock Elliott, mentors and friends Andrew Kershaw, Ken Roman, Gene Grayson, John Blaney, Bill Phillips, and Mike O'Brien, chief handyman of Ogilvy & Mather, who had moved my furniture ten times in twelve years.

Andrew Kershaw made a toast, and I was asked to respond. I could think only of the wish the Irish father had made on "Name That Tune" so many years before. I lifted my glass to the people I loved, who loved and supported me.

"May the road rise to meet you, may the wind be always at your back, and may the good Lord hold you in the palm of his hand."

P & G & Me

*C*harlie Moss, president of Wells, Rich, Greene, was the man who hired me. When he called, he told me I had been highly recommended by one of their art directors, Bob Cox, who had worked with me several years before at Ogilvy & Mather. This news surprised me, as Bob and I had quite different creative philosophies: He wanted brilliant, award-winning advertising; I wanted advertising that would sell the client's product. It was not always possible to give top priority to both objectives.

While Bob and I respected each other, and still do, I never expected that he would suggest me for a top spot in this most creative of creative agencies.

"Gee, Charlie," I said, "I'm not sure we should even waste each other's time talking at this point. I'm happy as a clam at Ogilvy, and I've been here for twelve years."

"Bob Cox says you are the best strategic thinker he's ever worked with," Charlie replied. "And that's exactly what we need right now on Procter & Gamble."

"I think you just said the magic words, Charlie." We made a date to meet at his office the following week. My head was spinning. Procter & Gamble, the marketer's marketer. It was tempting to dream of studying them from the inside.

A week later I sat in the dramatic lobby of Wells, Rich, Greene's offices on the twenty-eighth floor of the General Motors Building, admiring the view over Central Park, the spiral staircase connecting to the twenty-ninth floor, the expensive paintings on the walls, the mass of fresh flowers on the receptionist's desk. The wooden floors were highly polished, and oriental rugs were casually scattered at intervals. Compared to the businesslike atmosphere at Ogilvy & Mather, this was the Hollywood version of an advertising agency.

Charlie's secretary escorted me into his office, and I hoped my surprise didn't show. Ogilvy & Mather had accustomed me to executives in dark blue suits who wore suspenders. Behind the desk of this handsome office sat a kid in a sweater, his hair styled in a giant Afro. He looked up from a book he was reading, a copy of Roman and Maas's *How to Advertise.* "Hi," he said, extending his hand. "I'm Charlie Moss."

"Jane Moss," I answered, taking his hand. "No, Jane Maas."

Charlie looked at the reel of commercials I had created or supervised at Ogilvy & Mather, and asked if I would like to see a Wells, Rich, Greene reel. It really wasn't necessary, I told him. Everybody in advertising knew Wells was one of the hottest creative agencies in the country. Their campaign for Bic lighters, "Flick your Bic," was being used by every comic on television. Bob Hope commented about the energy crisis and ways in which people were conserving fuel. "The Statue of Liberty doesn't light her lamp anymore," he said. "She just stands there and flicks her Bic."

That's just one example of advertising campaigns by Wells, Rich, Greene that found their way into our national vocabulary. Two of the most famous were both for Alka-Seltzer: "Try it, you'll like it" and "I can't believe I ate the whole thing."

Charlie Moss told me candidly that the agency was not giving P & G the kind of strategic thinking that this client demanded. He did not tell me the as yet secret news that Procter & Gamble had removed Gleem toothpaste from the agency's account assignments. One of the ways in which Wells, Rich, Greene responded was by identifying and hiring some new creative people accustomed to working successfully within strategic limits.

Charlie asked me what sort of salary bracket I was in. He grinned, looking very much like a little boy. "We're very cheap," he warned. I named a figure that seemed to be high without being ridiculous. Charlie looked noncommittal, and ushered me out to the lobby, promising to call me the following week. I caught my heel on one of the oriental rugs, skittered in a 360-degree arc across the shiny floor, and ended up at his feet. Charlie looked down at me. "We lose more copywriters that way."

The next week passed without any call from Wells, Rich, Greene. "I guess they didn't like my reel," I told Michael. "Or maybe my price is too high."

After two weeks, I called Charlie's office. "I've, uh, I've been out of town," I stammered to his secretary, Noel. "I was, uh, just concerned that he might have left a message that I didn't receive."

"Oh no," Noel said cheerfully. "He hasn't tried to reach you."

"I'm really just as pleased," I told Michael. "I don't want to leave Ogilvy & Mather anyway."

Charlie called the next day and offered me the job. It came with the title of vice president, associate creative director, and the assignment to work on Prell shampoo and Safeguard deodorant soap. I called Charlie back at the end of the day and accepted. I would give Ogilvy & Mather notice, and start in four weeks.

In the car, I told Michael my news. "I knew they were going to offer you that job," he told me.

"But you didn't know I was going to accept," I countered.

"I knew from the first second," Michael said complacently.

"How?"

"Because you looked exactly the way you did when you were waiting for me to propose."

"Fink," I said huffily, knowing he was right.

While I was saying my good-byes and putting my accounts in order at Ogilvy & Mather, I began to spend lunch hours, evenings, and weekends working at Wells, Rich, Greene. There was an enormous amount of creative work to be done on both Prell and Safeguard over the summer months to produce commercials that would be on television by early fall. And the agency wanted to prove to P & G that they could deliver!

The same reasoning that led to my hiring also resulted in another recruitment from the Ogilvy & Mather ranks. Only a few weeks after I announced my departure, my old friend Charlie Fredericks, an executive vice president of Ogilvy, called to tell me he'd been offered the presidency of Wells, Rich, Greene. He was as startled as I was.

"I kept getting these telephone messages that a Mary Lawrence had called," he said. "I didn't know any Mary Lawrence, so I figured it was somebody looking for a job. Then the phone rang in my office, I picked it up and a secretary announced 'Mary Lawrence is calling.' And I said, 'Wait a minute, who the hell is Mary Lawrence?' And the secretary said 'Mary Wells Lawrence, chairman of Wells, Rich, Greene.'"

Mary told Charlie he had been suggested for the position, and she would like to meet with him, if he would like to meet with her. He did, and many weeks and many meetings later, Charlie officially became president of WRG. Charlie Moss, who'd been president before him, happily returned to the job he loved better than any other, that of executive creative director, vice chairman, and Mary's right-hand man.

It was inevitable that a few other Ogilvy & Mather account folks followed Charlie. Most of the top management at Ogilvy & Mather understood. (Andrew Kershaw, chairman, told me at lunch one day, "If I left to head up another agency, and nobody tried to come with me, I'd feel really hurt.") The only negative reaction at Wells, Rich, Greene was caused by a habit that all of us ex-Ogilvy types shared without realizing it. I overheard an account executive pass my office one day, muttering to a friend, "If one of them quotes David Ogilvy one more time today, I quit!"

My first meeting with the Procter & Gamble clients was sheer bliss. It began with the account executive reading the current copy strategy. This practice is rather like that of beginning a board meeting with an invocation. All P & G meetings at which creative work will be discussed begin with the Reading of the Strategy. I insist on using this tactic now at Muller Jordan Weiss. It does wonders to focus attention on the central issue, the objective of the advertising, not merely clever executions.

Creative work is highly subjective. It is perfectly normal and acceptable to present a storyboard or print layout that the client does not like. It is absolutely *unacceptable* to present creative work that is off strategy. If I were a client and my agency showed me executions that did not follow the strategy agreed upon, I would warn them once. Then I would fire them.

We discussed the Safeguard creative strategy for hours, and agreed to stick with it. However, my new partner, art director Arthur Kugelman, and I were asked to do a creative exploratory to see if we could outscore the current campaign. It positioned Safeguard as the soap that everybody in the family preferred, so it always ended up as "the smallest soap in the house."

"How about a continuing character," I suggested to Art. As I've mentioned, continuing characters can be extremely effective for the right products, and Procter & Gamble has had more than its share of successes. They include Mr. Whipple for Charmin, Rosie for Bounty, and Josephine the Plumber for Comet. Josephine was so terrific that Comet returned to her years later, reincarnated as the niece of Josephine.

Aaron Ehrlich, our director of broadcast production at Muller Jordan Weiss, has produced lots of "continuing character" commercials. Ehrlich says there are certain dead giveaways in any commercial that signal the "birth" of a continuing character. First of all, the character arrives in some conveyance that has his or her name plastered all over it. Second, if possible, the name appears on the character's T-shirt, overalls or uniform. And, finally, says Ehrlich, "if the name of the protagonist is invoked more than three times in the first ten seconds, you know you are in on the creation."

I always write a personality statement about the continuing character before I begin on the first script. Does this person take baths or showers, play golf or tennis, eat liver? We've written a detailed description of the cartoon character who is spokesman for Stroehmann Bread, the much-loved Grampa Stroehmann. I thought that no psychiatrist knew more about a patient than we did about Grampa. Then a new copywriter created a storyboard introducing a *Grandma* Stroehmann. Now we have to decide whether Grampa is a widower or simply a perennial bachelor.

Continuing characters are not a guarantee of success, and I've had a few disasters with them. The most disappointing was for a new product, Industrial Strength Drano. Instead of taking a more usual route, I suggested we use Frankie Fontaine, remembered as a frequent customer at the bar in the Jackie Gleason Show, and known for his unique wheezing laugh. We established Frank as the owner of a greasy-spoon restaurant who always had terrible drain problems until he discovered new Industrial Strength Drano. "Is it strong?" he was asked by one customer.

"Strong?" he replied. "Yesterday a meatball got stuck in my drain, and this new Drano is so strong, today that meatball ended up in the Chinese laundry next door." He snorted with laughter.

The TV audience did not. The Burke score was something under 5 percent. And, with hindsight, I can agree there is good reason for it. When people have problems that lead them to buy Industrial Strength anything, they need assurance that the product will work, not buffoonery.

However, I was convinced a continuing character just might work for Safeguard. How about a woman from Texas, complete with accent, who ran a dude ranch and provided all her dusty, weary guests with nothing but Safeguard.

Art Kugelman thought about the possibilities of this campaign. "Hack," he said.

How about a relevant celebrity? I reminded Art how well Patricia Neal had worked for Maxim, how long Robert Young as Dr. Marcus Welby had worked for Sanka.

True, I told Art, the word "relevant" is key. Unless the personality is in some way connected with the product, the celebrity will overwhelm the message and the Burke score will be dismal. I have often relied upon measurements such as TV-Q, which give statistics not only on how well known and how well liked a performer is, but how that performer would be perceived as spokesperson in a given category. I once wanted to use Sophia Loren on behalf of a food product. Research showed she was well known and liked by women. However, even though she had just published a cookbook, nobody believed she knew anything about food.

So, Art, how about a relevant celebrity for Safeguard deodorant soap?

Art mused. "No celebrity will admit he sweats."

I played my ace. A demonstration commercial! Television is a visual medium, and nothing works better than proving to the viewer why your product is better. Think of some of the most memorable commercials you have ever seen. Chances are at least one of them is a demonstration. The gorilla jumping up and down on the Tourister luggage. The car using Shell going farther than the other car and crashing triumphantly through the paper barrier. And my favorite, Ali MacGraw, before she became famous, swimming in a paper bikini to demonstrate the strength of a new product for International Paper. And then, at the end of the commercial, taking the bikini off under water and tossing it toward the camera to show it was easily disposable. Proof that demonstration commercials don't have to be dull.

A demonstration commercial for Safeguard? Art allowed we might do something quite creative. We needed only to find the right demonstration.

I sat in the bathtub making Safeguard lather until my skin shriveled. Michael came home one night and found me reading in bed, a glob of Safeguard on one cheek, a glob of a competitive deodorant soap on the other. I explained that I was hoping the other brand would get hard and dry, while Safeguard stayed soft and full of lather.

Both brands dried at the same speed, and all I ended up with was a rash.

The account group at Wells, Rich, Greene and the Safeguard brand group at Procter pushed us harder. Safeguard was under attack from a new deodorant soap called Coast. It was launched under a strategy of freshness, positioning Coast as the soap that gets you going in

the morning. The commercials all began with sleepy people who were suddenly galvanized into action. The spots
were funny, too, written by some of the talented folks at
Doyle Dane Bernbach. (I remember one commercial that
showed a man reluctantly getting out of bed on a rainy
day. Revived by Coast, he was whistling, putting on his
coat. His wife eyed the monsoon outside. "How are you
going to get to work?" she asked. "Backstroke," he answered.)

Most laymen are surprised to learn that the maker of
Coast is none other than Procter & Gamble. Yet most successful package goods companies compete with themselves. Johnson Wax makes Pledge and Favor furniture
polishes. General Foods spends large amounts of money
to convince us to drink Sanka brand decaffeinated coffee,
and probably equally large amounts to convince us that
Brim decaffeinated tastes better.

The philosophy is simple. Why allow another company
to bring out a successful competitive product when you
can do it yourself? At Procter & Gamble, brand groups
working on rival products are as aggressive about beating
the brand down the hall as they are one from Colgate or
Lever Brothers.

Top management discourages sharing information, although it won't let the rivalry go so far as to endanger
any one product. The Coast brand group was right
around the corner from us at Safeguard. We greeted
each other politely in the hallways and vowed to bury
them.

A demonstration commercial for Safeguard? "Good
idea," said Art Kugelman. But we couldn't come up with
one.

Now Art had an idea. How about a campaign featuring
famous detectives, like Charlie Chan and Sherlock
Holmes, who would track down the evidence leading to
the reason Safeguard was always the smallest soap in the

house? I spent nights reading detective stories to get the tone right, and we presented three or four storyboards.

The brand group turned them down flat. Later, Norman Levy, P & G's resident guru for commercials-that-have-failed-in-the-past, explained why. "Every year, at least one creative team from one agency comes up with the idea of using famous detectives. Oh, it's a cute idea," he consoled us. "It's just that we've a made a couple of those commercials and they never work."

Art Kugelman and I ended up creating new commercials for the successful "smallest soap in the house" campaign, including one that introduced a larger bar of Safeguard, and another that launched a new fresh scent. The commercials scored well, the account group and the brand group were happy, and the rash faded from my cheek.

We were on exactly the same timetable for Prell shampoo, rushing to get a commercial into test markets. The new campaign, based on an improved Prell that kept hair smelling fresh for twenty-four hours, had just been launched and seemed to be working. However, P & G, like many other marketers, feels safer when a backup campaign is running in a few cities.

Creative teams that work together well walk in and out of each other's heads without knocking. When the harness fits, neither partner knows by the time the commercial is finished who is responsible for what. That's the way Ken Roman and I wrote *How to Advertise*. Art directors write copy; copywriters dream up visuals.

Art and I were on a collision course from the beginning. He was aiming for commercials that would charm, amuse, win awards, and get talked about. There's nothing wrong with that. I was aiming for commercials with high Burke scores. There's nothing wrong with that either. We simply disagreed on executions.

We created three storyboards for Prell on a strategy of

"healthy-looking hair." Two of them were truly Art's babies. One, called "Beach," featured a young woman talking about the current fads in shampoos, explaining why she was sticking with Prell. The other, "Hats Off," showed lots of beautiful women removing their hats to reveal shiny, bouncy hair, hair that was "alive and kicky."

"My" commercial was called "Baby-sitter." It opened with an attractive young mother complaining to her baby-sitter about her stringy, limp hair. The baby-sitter displayed her own shiny locks and suggested that Mom try Prell. Dissolve to shampoo sequence. Dissolve again. The husband entered, came upon his wife from behind and, due to her transformed hair, took her to be the baby-sitter. She turned, he expressed astonishment and delight, they embraced.

We presented to the assistant brand manager. He didn't like "Beach" or "Hats Off." He did like "Baby-sitter." "But it needs a reason why," he said. "It needs a demonstration."

We moved on to the brand manager. "The only one I'd spend money filming is 'Baby-sitter,'" he said. "But I yearn for a demonstration." (P & G apparently teaches its brand people that it is impolite to say "I want." At P & G, brand people always "yearn.")

The associate advertising manager agreed with everything that had been said. Only when we reached the heights of the advertising manager himself did matters change. He looked thoughtfully at the storyboards for "Beach" and "Hats Off." "Well," he said, "you've got one that knocks the fads, and maybe that'll work. And you've got one that's alive and kicky and full of pretty hair. And maybe that'll work. So I think we should put them on film."

Art was so pleased he almost hugged me. The vice president continued. "The one I think is your winner is the 'Baby-sitter,'" he concluded. "But I yearn for a demonstration. In fact, I think you should add a demonstration to all three commercials."

Art gagged, and we went back to the drawing board to dream up a demonstration. This time we succeeded, with an animated sequence showing how Prell removed dirt and oil.

So we produced all three commercials. "The most expendable money," say the P & G folks, "is the money spent on producing commercials." They don't like to *waste* money, either. In fact, they were the first big advertiser to insist that all commercials be filmed in 16mm, less expensive than the traditional 35mm, used for feature films. Directors howl in protest, but I know even experts cannot tell the difference.

P & G would rather film three commercials and hope that one of them will score a home run on the Burke tests than weed out likely prospects prematurely. Compared to the money they make in the nation's supermarkets, production dollars are peanuts.

"Beach" and "Hats Off" failed in Burke testing. "Babysitter" scored better than any Prell commercial had in years, and the verbatims showed that viewers remembered every nuance of the plot, every word about Prell. They even liked the demonstration! I floated around the agency, queen of the roost. For about two weeks.

Wells, Rich, Greene had one of its regular creative reviews, attended by all the top brass of the agency, including Mary Wells Lawrence. The three Prell commercials were screened, and the results of the Burke tests announced. Mary asked that the "Baby-sitter" commercial be shown again. It was. I waited for my full measure of praise.

Mary looked at Charlie Moss, sitting on one side of her, then at Charlie Fredericks, sitting on the other. "I'm afraid I don't like that commercial at all," Mary said. "It seems so . . . expected."

High Burke scores aren't enough for Mary. She wants
every commercial that is created by her agency to have
"star quality," to cause a stir. She didn't think "Baby-sitter" hit that mark.

Only one week later, Charlie Moss came to tell me
gently that I was invited to step off the Prell account. It
was one of the lowest moments of my life. I called Michael and asked him to meet me for a drink after work.

"Have they made you president already?" he chuckled.

"Don't laugh," I said. "I think I may be fired."

I should have known better. Mary Wells Lawrence had
other ideas for me. Let me tell you about Mary. Every
advertising agency should have one. So should every corporation.

She is, first of all, a superb creative thinker and a marketing genius. It was Mary's idea to paint the Braniff
planes in brilliant colors and dress the stewardesses in
Pucci uniforms. It was Mary's idea to focus on a variety of
tummies for the famous Alka-Seltzer commercial, "No
matter what shape your stomach's in."

Is she tough? Not in the way that question is usually
meant. Katherine Graham, publisher of the Washington
Post, gave a speech discussing some of the myths that sur-
round successful women. She said that right after Mary
Wells founded her agency, word went around that she
smoked cigars and swore like a trooper. Mary does neither. In fact, I have never heard her raise her voice.

However, Mary is *tough-minded,* as any person, man or
woman, who runs a large advertising agency has to be.
Mary does not demand any more of those working for
her than she demands of herself. I have seen her at midnight, after listening to the three-hour rehearsal of an
agency new-business presentation, explaining softly to
various presenters what was wrong and adding, "Now,
let's do it again. Right."

She is a spellbinding presenter and, unlike some

agency people, who make lots of new business presentations but hate being on their feet, Mary adores it. So does Charlie Moss. So do I. All three of us started out headed for careers on the stage, not in advertising. Does this have something to do with our enjoyment of being "on stage"? I think so.

Mary delights in rewarding services well rendered. My first special "thank you" from her, for help in researching a speech, was one single sprig of lily-of-the-valley in a tiny vase. Not easy to come by in February. "It reminded me of you," Mary wrote me in the accompanying note. Other gifts followed over the next years, always hand selected by Mary, always with a handwritten note, always with that special "Mary touch."

She is generous with praise as well. Once she wrote a memo to her entire top management team, some dozen people. It began, "In the past year Jane Maas's reputation has been flowering to such a degree in New York City that it is almost impossible for me to go anywhere without being attacked by rapturous admirers of hers." Mary didn't have to write that note, but she wanted to. I try to emulate that generosity of spirit in my job now, realizing how much a few words can mean.

People often ask me if Mary really works at heading Wells, Rich, Greene or if she is more a token chairman. Nobody at that agency works harder. Mary is there every day, unless she is visiting clients out of town, except for the month of July, when she and her family go to their villa at St. Jean Cap Ferrat in Southern France. Even there, Mary entertains clients almost the entire time. If you think it's easy to entertain almost nonstop, even with the best of household help, think again. It's exhausting.

While Harding Lawrence was operating Braniff in Texas and Mary was running the agency in New York, she logged more miles than most pilots. Mary boarded a plane almost every Friday night to spend the weekend with her husband in Texas, returning Sunday night or early Monday morning. I learned from Mary to make good use of that precious time on planes. A short trip is a wonderful time to go through mail, read reports you've been postponing. A long one is ideal for writing a speech, a white paper, a position statement.

When Mary is picked up at the airport, she always has her mail delivered. By the time she is back in her office, she has sifted through it, arranged it in terms of priorities, and jotted answers to the most important requests. We can't all have the luxury of limousines to meet us, but the principle holds. Use time while traveling to catch up on work.

The only exception to this rule is time spent traveling to and from vacations. Never take work with you on these occasions. Read voraciously of the old and of the new. I confess to Jane Austen and science fiction.

Another great trick I learned from Mary is the charm—and efficiency—of lunch at one's office. Nothing consumes more time and energy and adds more calories than a restaurant luncheon, especially if, like Mary, one is called on to entertain clients, prospective clients or colleagues almost every day.

Mary normally invites guests to her elegant office, where good food is served on fine china, good wine poured into fine crystal. The guests are so enchanted by the ambiance and by the hostess that few notice Mary is sipping Perrier and nibbling crudités.

Don't misunderstand. The Kriendler-Berns clan of the "21" Club and Tom Margittai and Paul Kovi of Four Seasons are among my dearest friends, and I love their restaurants, lunch at them frequently, and have dinners there with Michael almost every week. As I've mentioned, "21" is a great restaurant for dieters. So is Four Seasons, which has low-calorie, salt-free "spa" cuisine. Try the world's tiniest bay scallops, on a bed of leaf spinach, napped in a purée of tomatoes. Heaven.

Soon after I joined her agency, Mary Wells Lawrence began to pay me the greatest possible compliment. I became her "stand-in" on many occasions. One of the most exciting committees I served on in her stead was the Business Council for the Equal Rights Amendment. The CEO of almost every Fortune 500 company was on the Council. Polly Bergen, fine actress and astute businesswoman, was co-chair together with Coy Eklund, chairman of Equitable Life. The League of Women Voters sponsored the council and cheered it on.

One day, we were invited to Washington to join President and Mrs. Carter for lunch, and to hear the President speak on behalf of the Equal Rights Amendment. Guards stopped me at the White House gate and asked for identification. I produced my American Express card. It seems the White House doesn't honor American Express. They asked for my passport. I told them I didn't usually travel between New York and Washington with a passport. "Okay," the guards said. "Driver's license." I confessed that I didn't have one because I didn't know how to drive. An *American citizen* who didn't know how to drive! Clearly, their expressions indicated, they were dealing here with some anarchist. Just as they were about to haul me away for frisking, a friend inside the gate vouched for me and the guards let me through.

We assembled in the East Room, where Lincoln had once lain in state. And, for the first time in my life, I experienced the shiver of awe that must be shared by every American, Democrat or Republican, when a voice announces, "Ladies and gentlemen, the President of the United States." I reminded myself that I was there because Mary Wells Lawrence felt I could represent her at the highest levels.

A few days after the Prell debacle, she invited me to

her office for tea and a long talk. She has that rare quality of concentration; when she focuses on you, you think you are the most important person in the world to her. And at that moment, you are.

"You are a generalist," Mary told me. "There are not many people like you. I believe you can do anything you want to do, and I think you would be superb on the account management side. How would you like to go to work on the little account that's just starting up for New York State?"

I advise my young friends in the advertising business or any other to expect some bloody noses in the climb up the ladder, but to look for any opportunity to turn adversity into triumph. That "little account" became one of the most famous campaigns in advertising history. It swept me right along with it.

The "I Love New York" Experience

*J*ust imagine a first meeting between a new client and its advertising agency. The client admits there are a few problems with the product he wants the agency to sell. People consider it dirty, hard to use, expensive and downright dangerous. Sales have been declining for nine years. Add to this the fact that the client has had his credit rating suspended by Standard & Poor's and is on the verge of bankruptcy. Most agencies would run for the hills. But that was exactly the situation of New York State, as described by Charlie Moss, when it first came to the agency in 1976. From this inauspicious beginning grew the most successful tourism program ever created and certainly one of the most famous advertising campaigns of the decade. It has been said that success has many fathers, and "I Love New York" has its full share of them. But I am its only mother.

The campaign is a classic case history in the use of market research to point the way to a positioning and strategy. The creative executions are also advertising classics. The goals were all set in advance, and all were achieved. The only unexpected result of the program was the fact that I ended up running the state wedding for New York's governor.

Wells, Rich, Greene accepted the challenge of helping

to turn around the economy of the state, and the program was put under the care of a marketing genius, the late Marty Stern, the "founding father" of "I Love New York." The agency urged the Department of Commerce not to put even a penny of its tiny $200,000 budget into immediate advertising, but to fund the most sophisticated market research ever done by a state. "We don't know who is coming to New York," Marty told the legislative committee in Albany. "We don't know why they are coming. Even more important, we don't know why they are *not.*"

An outside research organization conducted 1,800 telephone and mail interviews in eight states, including New York State, and two Canadian provinces. The research findings were astounding.

First, New York State and New York City were two totally different products, with appeal to two different audiences. Traditionally, they had been advertised together, a major marketing blunder. Clearly, from now on, we would have to advertise them separately.

New York State's biggest problem was lack of awareness. When respondents in the study were asked what destination first popped into their minds when thinking about a vacation, only 8 percent mentioned New York. Yet further probing revealed 13 percent had actually vacationed there. It's like inviting guests to your home to find, a year later, they don't remember ever being there at all. (Were you disagreeable, or just dull?)

Yet the research showed New York had appeal to visitors. For the state, outdoor beauty and recreation were foremost. For New York City, one attraction stood head and shoulders above all others for attracting tourists the first time and drawing them back again and again: Broadway theater.

The agency and the Department of Commerce put together a two-hour presentation, including several hundred slides, that convinced the New York State legislature that tourism was potentially a big money-maker. They voted to invest $4.3 million in an advertising campaign.

Hugh Carey, who will go down in history as one of New York's great governors, was a driving force behind the program. When the budget passed, he invited some of the key agency people to visit him at the Executive Mansion in Albany. Mary Lawrence saw this as a splendid chance to see the beauties of New York State and chartered a helicopter. "Vell," said Marty Stern, in his soft German accent, "there go the profits for the year."

"Give me a great advertising campaign," Hugh Carey asked Mary Lawrence. "I want people to love New York as much as I do. Give me advertising that will make them feel that way."

The new budget was approved on April 1. We had to be on television advertising summer vacations in New York State no later than the third week in May, and even that was late for holiday decision making. The schedule meant creation of a new advertising campaign, approvals, revisions, filming and editing, in just seven weeks. A normal schedule would demand about four months. But summer wouldn't wait.

Because the New York State assignment was so important, Mary Lawrence asked Charlie Moss to take it over himself. Charlie is responsible for more award-winning campaigns than you can shake a stick at. Do you remember "The end of the plain plane" for Braniff? That was Charlie Moss. "Flick your Bic?" Charlie again. "Midasize it!" Charlie.

Charlie Moss created the "I Love New York" campaign. The storyboard showed lots of people fishing, riding horseback, swimming, camping; all in New York State. The fisherman said, "I'm from New Hampshire, but I love New York." The last vignette was a camper who declared, "I'm from Brooklyn, but I *loooove* New York." The

promise of the commercial was, "If you love the out-
doors, you'll love New York."

Our clients were Commissioner of Commerce John
Dyson and Senior Deputy Commissioner William Doyle.
Dyson, a brilliant verbal gymnast in his midthirties, was a
splendid Carey appointee. He had reached out for his
friend and fellow Vietnam veteran, marketing whiz Bill
Doyle. They were an iconoclastic team that never settled
for anything but first class. Doyle took one look at the
storyboard and said GO!

It was spring in New York City, but still winter in the
Adirondacks when we filmed the commercial in early
May. The first scene showed the fisherman, standing hip
deep in water, casting for trout. Anyone who has ever
been on location knows the agonizing, "hurry up and
wait" delays that occur. We filmed take after take. The
fisherman stood out in the water so long that he caught a
fish. Not easy, especially with no bait on his hook.

During helicopter photography, the crew flew over
most of New York State, shooting scenery. One morning,
it swooped down to get a closer look at a gorgeous blonde
sunning herself in the nude. We learned the day we
screened the commercial for the press that the house belonged to Sun Yung Moon. They sent a delegation to the
press conference to make sure that particular bit of
footage was not part of the finished spot.

Enter another "father" of the "I Love New York" campaign, music man Steve Karmen, known as "the king of
the jingle jungle." Steve looked at the film footage, and
went away to meditate. He could have zeroed in on the
outdoor theme and written a lyric like "New York, the
outdoor state." Instead, something about the repetition of
"I Love New York" caught his imagination and his ear.
The song that became the campaign theme was born.
Within a year, "I Love New York" was an international
hit. It is now the official song of the state of New York,

and for a while it was even number two on the Japanese Hit Parade.

The next "father," Milton Glaser, created the logo,

I♥NY

which is perhaps the most imitated logo in the world. I have seen it everywhere. "I Love Paris." "I Love Osaka." "I Love Okefenokee." A bumper sticker with the logo was once pasted on the Great Wall of China. Dear gentle Milton charged the state an honorarium of $1,000 for that logo. It is worth untold millions.

Not many people know that a conscious decision was made, early on, *not* to license the logo, *not* to charge a fee for its use. The agency, the Department of Commerce, and Governor Carey all agreed that the more it appeared, the higher the awareness of New York State would be. We wanted every tourist attraction, from the biggest hotel chain to the tiniest museum, to afford to use it. The decision was right.

We were ready to go on television the third week in May, late for summer-vacation planning. To make up for the delay, we poured on the frequency. For five weeks, we ran the commercial at an almost unprecedented 200 Gross Rating Points every week. This media jargon means that our target audience was seeing the "I Love New York" commercial almost every time they turned on a television set.

The response was immediate. Overnight, gas stations reported they were out of New York State maps. And when New York City cab drivers, a notoriously cynical lot, blossomed forth with "I Love New York" bumper stickers, we knew we had a hit.

A second wave of research at the end of the summer proved the advertising was working. Our long-term plan had called for the program to increase awareness of New York State as a vacation destination by ten percentage

points in five years. Instead, we had raised it by six percentage points in *five weeks*. No advertising story demon-
strates more clearly the power of television to generate
immediate awareness.

The research also told us that 90 percent of the people
in our target markets were aware of the "I Love New
York" slogan. Not bad, when you consider that only 89
percent of Americans know that Christopher Columbus
discovered this country.

At this point, Dolores Coyne Zahn entered my life, as
secretary, confidante, conscience and aide-de-camp. Dolores wasn't even looking for a secretarial job in New York
City. She'd made the trek in from Brightwaters, Long Island, just to keep her daughter, Mary, company while
Mary went job-hunting. The head of Personnel at Wells,
Rich, Greene knew I was in the market for a secretary.
(My last secretary wanted to be a copywriter and I helped
her put a portfolio together. She landed a writing job at
Compton. The secretary before that wanted to be a production assistant, and I helped her find a spot working
for a senior producer.) Now I really wanted a secretary
who wanted to be a secretary. Enter Dolores.

We had a brief interview. "I'm not sure I'm right for
this job," Dolores said candidly. "My experience has been
working for the Psychiatric Clinic of Catholic Charities in
Long Island. I function best with disturbed people."

"You'll be perfect in advertising," I assured her. And she
was. For the next seven years, Dolores calmed me down,
steered me through shoals I didn't perceive and protected
me from villains I was too naïve to spot. In 1984, when
Norman Zahn decided it was time to retire, he said to
Dolores, "Well, you have two choices. You can come to
Florida with me, or you can stay in New York with Jane."

Dolores paused for a long moment. "I'm thinking," she
told Norman.

Dolores was a great addition to "I Love New York." She set

up an incredible system, double-filing every document under its subject matter as well as in chronological order. She'd been with me just one month when Personnel realized I was the only person in the entire agency, except for Mary Wells Lawrence, who was not sharing a secretary with anyone else. They descended to confront Dolores with the news that she would have to take on another account person.

Dolores shook the "chron book" under their noses. "Jane Maas wrote the equivalent of *Gone With the Wind* last month," she said, "and I have no doubt she'll write it again this month and the month after. Whoever else you give me to look after had better be a good typist." Dolores won.

In September, Commissioner Bill Doyle suggested that I join him on a tour of all ten regions of New York State, presenting a series of seminars on how regional and local tourist attractions could advertise and promote themselves more effectively. I put together a thirty-minute slide presentation, "Better Advertising and Promotion for Your Money."

Bill and I, and our little staff of press and audiovisual assistants, visited ten cities in five days. I gave the talk eleven times, twice in Buffalo as a result of scheduling problems. We started in Albany, then attempted to fly to Plattsburgh, the northernmost tip of the state. An early blizzard forced us to land and drive the rest of the way. ("Hell," natives of the Adirondacks told us, "this is just a little dusting.")

We pressed on across the state, which loomed larger than Texas, to Buffalo, then were taken in a big recreational vehicle, where I could steal a nap, down to the beautiful but little-known southwestern region of Chautauqua. Plus the Finger Lakes, Rochester, Syracuse, and lots of points in between.

For one leg of the grand tour, a wondrous guide volunteered to be host and driver. Don Hogan, for many years head of the New York State Travel and Vacation Association, is a giant of a man, with appetite to match. As we drove from Jamestown toward the Finger Lakes, Don stopped at a local market for provisions. Bill and I watched in awe as he returned to the car. He might have been stocking a Conestoga wagon for the long journey west. Don opened his trunk and unfurled a large white piece of material. "I never travel without a tablecloth," he told us as he spread the cloth over himself, the front seat, and part of Bill Doyle's left leg. Don began with a sack of powdered doughnuts. Powdered sugar filled the car, while Bill, the most fastidious of men, huddled in his corner. Don ate his way across the state, chatting with dozens of people on his CB. His code name, not unexpectedly, is "Big Hoagie." (I became "Little Red.")

Since that eventful trip, Don went on a diet, stopped drinking the rich local Chautauqua wine, and lost one hundred pounds. The only thing unchanging about him is his love for New York State.

Every time I gave the presentation, I noticed that our audiences listened attentively enough when I spoke about how to do better print ads and radio commercials. When I started talking about creating better brochures, suddenly pencils came out, and people began making lengthy notes. By the end of the week, it was clear that a book was lurking in this topic. Not everybody has enough money to advertise, but just about every tourism-related activity produces brochures. During the following year, I wrote the book. It's called *Better Brochures, Catalogs and Mailing Pieces*. All the royalties go to Bucknell University, as do those from *How to Advertise*.

The final speech of the tour was given on Friday evening in Bear Mountain. I didn't realize until I stepped in the car taking me to New York how exhausted I was. I slept all the way home, slept through the night, then got up to pack for a trip with Michael to Rome and Florence.

I slept the entire flight away and arrived in Rome ready for anything. "You look pretty chipper for somebody who's just arrived in her eleventh city," Michael said.

"Maybe," I said. "But in *this* city I don't have to make a speech."

Our trip was full of "Maas weather" and "Maas luck." We jogged from our hotel, the Hassler, on top of the Spanish Steps, across to St. Peter's, and around the Trastevere section. Here, we discovered one of our favorite restaurants in all the world, Sabatini's; one of our favorite dishes, *zuppa di pesce;* and one of our favorite waiters, Sergio. When you're in Rome, go, ask for Sergio and tell him the Maases sent you.

En route from Siena to Florence, we "shunpiked" to visit some of the Tuscan vineyards. It was early afternoon, and Michael was ready for lunch. Was there anything in the Michelin Guide that looked promising? "Where are we?" I asked.

Michael pointed to a sign: CASTELLINA IN CHIANTI, 3 KM.

"I don't know, hon," I said dubiously, opening the Michelin to the name of the town. "I've never heard of it." The Michelin people, however, had. The red symbol that indicated a lovely quiet setting told us about the elegant old Villa Casalecchi. We drove in, parked the car, opened the great wooden door. Nobody was around. "Hello," we called. "*Buon giorno!* Hello!" By the time we entered the dining room, a few startled staffers appeared. This was the day before the villa closed for the season, they told us in Italian. We were indeed their only visitors. "Could you give us something to eat?" we asked. They could, but warned us we would have to take potluck. Half an hour later, we sat in solitary splendor in the high-beamed dining room, eating roast chicken, drinking one of the great red Chiantis from their famed cellar, and being invited back the next year.

We drove on to Florence, and looked out from the balcony of our room in the Excelsior Hotel toward the church of San Miniato al Monte, where the sun was setting. "Let me throw some cold water on my face, and we can run up to San Miniato before it's dark," said the cheerleader.

"We can go to San Miniato tomorrow," Michael said. "Relax."

"Spoilsport," I said. "*Avanti!*" I was applying the cold water when I heard the popping of a champagne cork. Michael knew one sure way to subvert my best sightseeing motives. We had champagne on the balcony and watched the sun set over San Miniato.

"Who is right, as usual?" Michael wanted to know.

We left Florence on a Wednesday morning. More accurately, we *tried* to leave Florence. Michael takes a "God will provide" attitude toward many things, including gasoline, so our tank was almost empty as we looked for a nearby gas station that morning. The one near the hotel was closed. So was the next one. And the next. I hailed a taxi and pleaded, "*Benzina?*"

The driver pointed at his taxi and shook his head sadly. "*Diesel.*"

One more gas station, also closed. I got out of the car, and went into a carpenter's shop next to it. "*Benzina!*" I implored.

"*Non c'e benzina,*" the carpenter told me.

I gasped. "*Non c'e benzina in Firenze?*"

The carpenter shook his head. "*Non c'e benzina in tutta Italia!*"

Italy was having a gasoline crisis, and all gas stations were closed on Wednesdays. Except, we learned gratefully from a policeman minutes later, for one on the *autostrada* right outside of Florence. We filled the tank, and Michael calculated we could make it as far as Rome on one tankful. I remembered this lesson a year or two later when the United States was suffering its own gasoline shortage. It threatened to cut down severely on tourists driving around New York State, so we invented the "Tankful Tours," a brochure describing trips visitors could make on just one tankful of gas.

By the time we returned from Italy, summer was well over, and it was time to turn our attention to increasing tourism to New York City. We knew that Broadway theater was the carrot to lure visitors, and, as a solution to visitors' concerns over "big city hassle," we worked with hotels, theaters, and other attractions to create tour packages.

Charlie Moss worked with his old friend, art director and film director Stan Dragoti. They developed a storyboard using the casts from current Broadway hits, all singing "I Love New York." Bill Doyle knew it was a winner. So did Harvey Sabinson, executive director of the League of New York Theaters and Producers. The delightful Harvey, who had previously been one of the most successful theatrical press agents in history, knew very well what a television campaign could do for ticket sales.

Charlie and Stan saw dozens of shows, looking for exactly the right few seconds to film. They huddled with the people from the League to make sure we wouldn't include a show that might close before we opened.

Most of the producers we contacted were pleased to be part of the commercial, and the performers went cheerfully along with the decision. There was one holdout. Yul Brynner, starring in *The King and I,* declined. Through his agent, we thanked him politely and said we had more than enough shows. Brynner's agent soon realized his client was going to be the only major star on Broadway *not* appearing in the commercial. Next day we received a telephone call. Mr. Brynner would appear after all. Having him was such a coup we couldn't even pretend reluctance.

We allowed four days for the filming, since so many people were involved. The casts included *Grease, Annie, The Wiz, A Chorus Line,* Hume Cronyn and Jessica Tandy from *The Gin Game, The King and I,* and Frank Langella as Dracula, who ended the commercial with the words, "I love New York . . . especially in the evening," then turned away from camera with a swirl of his cloak.

The third day of filming, we woke to one of the worst blizzards that ever hit New York. I panicked, knowing we were shooting *A Chorus Line,* the Cronyns, and the unpredictable Mr. Brynner with all the children from *The King and I.* At Wells, Rich, Greene, only 8 of the 439 employees managed to stagger in. (I was one of them.) Over at the set on Eighth Avenue, every single actor we expected arrived. And arrived on time.

The talent in that commercial was worth millions of dollars. Yet every actor, famous or unknown, worked for scale (the minimum daily wage), and they all waived residual payments for the cause of "I Love New York." That's *love!*

The commercial went on air, fittingly enough, on Valentine's Day. Public relations for the program then were handled by Bobby Zarem, whom *Time* magazine described with praise as "Mr. Flack." Bobby persuaded one of his clients, the Tavern on the Green, to host a luncheon for the casts of the Broadway shows, assorted VIPs, and state and city officials. Somehow, he managed to get Governor Hugh Carey, Lieutenant-Governor Mary Anne Krupsak, and Mayor Ed Koch smiling together while they cut a Valentine cake. Since no one of the three was especially fond of the others at that point, it was one of Bobby's greatest coups.

The Broadway spot created such a stir that all three networks had television crews out the next day, filming the long lines of people queuing up for Broadway tickets, particularly for shows included in the commercial. Frank

Langella became a matinee idol overnight. And fourteen thousand people called the toll-free 800 number within the first three days to ask for more information about Broadway tour packages.

Commissioner of Commerce John Dyson left the supervision of the tourism program very much to Bill Doyle. He did involve himself in the Economic Development program, aimed at persuading businesses already in New York State to stay here, as well as attracting out-of-state companies to establish themselves in New York.

The budget for this campaign was tiny, compared to that for tourism, but our target audience was a special one: chief executive officers and other high-ranking decision makers. The way to reach them was chiefly print media, such as business magazines and *The Wall Street Journal.*

Market research, again, pointed the way to the strategy and the campaign. The research firm of Yankelovich, Skelly, and White conducted a study that showed us even the most sophisticated business leaders were not aware of recent state tax reforms. Further, the state government was considered "faceless" and unresponsive.

Wells, Rich, Greene wanted to give the Department of Commerce a "face," that of Commissioner John Dyson. Photographer Francesco Scavullo took John's photograph, and he soon appeared as spokesman in a compelling print advertisement.

Some members of the state legislature bristled, feeling John might be using this advertising to pave the way for a run for public office. A special legislative committee hearing was convened in Albany to discuss deleting the photo from the advertisement. John Dyson, a man known more for his wit than his humility, showed up to protest the issue by wearing a Lone Ranger mask. Of course, the episode made newspapers all over the country.

Despite the Dyson controversy, we began year two of

the "I Love New York" program with incredible momentum. The New York State legislature looked over the figures for the first year. For every dollar spent on advertising, the program was generating an additional seven dollars in tax revenues to the state and local communities. The advertising budget for the first year had been just over four million. For the second year, the program was voted a budget of ten million dollars! At Wells, Rich, Greene we opened champagne.

We filmed more commercials for the state, featuring the wonders of its lakes and mountains. And more for New York City. Producers now clamored to have their shows included in the spot. One famous producer, who shall be nameless, called and offered me house seats for every performance if we would include his musical, which had not yet opened. I explained that we had a firm rule: Only established hits with enough advance sales to guarantee a long run could be filmed. The producer exploded in rage, and threatened to sue me. I turned him over to Fred Jacobs, vice chair, comptroller, attorney, and holy terror of Wells, Rich, Greene.

Fred could make management supervisors tremble and assistant account executives weep. One night, I caught both barrels from him. After the Lone Ranger episode, Fred warned all of us on "I Love New York" to be careful. Even though the support of the campaign was bipartisan, the press was now on the lookout for stories. Woe betide anyone at Wells, Rich, Greene who might generate one.

Art director Bob Mussachio had just completed a new print advertisement inviting visitors to camp in New York State's mountains. There wasn't time to take a photograph, so Bob found a "stock" photo, and had it retouched to clear up a blurry greenish-blue area that made a lake look muddy. The advertisement ran in newspapers across the state.

One enterprising reporter who knew the area saw something puzzling. He climbed the mountain that appeared in the photo, and looked down toward a greenish-blue *meadow*. We had innocently created a lake where none existed. The reporter christened it "Lake Dyson" and tried to reach Mary Wells Lawrence. Somehow, he was put through to the home of Fred Jacobs.

Just before midnight, our phone rang at home, waking me up. (Michael and I consider it a feat to stay up for the ten o'clock news.) Fred roared at me so loudly that he woke Michael. Michael listened for about ten seconds, then grabbed the telephone from my hand. "I don't know who you are, or why you're calling at this hour," Michael said, "but nobody shouts that way at my wife." He hung up.

This may have been the first time anybody ever hung up on Fred Jacobs. Our telephone rang seconds later. Michael answered. Fred Jacobs, a pussycat at heart, is also a man of charm and humor. "Shouting?" he asked. "Was I shouting? I can't believe that, it's so unlike me." Fred and Michael began a mutual-admiration society that endures.

The most people who ever yelled at me simultaneously were almost all the more than one hundred owners of New York ski areas. Betsy Boyd, a staff member of the Department of Commerce in charge of the ski program, convinced lots of the ski areas to run advertisements in a special ski edition of the New York *Times*. New York State would run a big "umbrella" ad, the ski areas would run smaller ads and, all together, we would "own" an entire page or two. I helped Betsy make dozens and dozens of calls, volunteering free copywriting help to those areas that needed it. We worked for about two months to pull it off.

The Sunday morning of the special edition, I opened the Travel Section in anticipation. There they were, dozens and dozens of individual ski areas. Only one thing was missing. There was no ad from the Department of Commerce. In my eagerness to help Betsy, I simply never told the Traffic Department to place the order.

The second New York City commercial was, if anything, even more spectacular than the first. We used the city itself as a backdrop. Beverly Sills and company sang "I Love New York" in Lincoln Center. The Rockettes tapped and sang in the skating rink at Rockefeller Center. Sandy Duncan as Peter Pan flew across the skyline at the foot of the Brooklyn Bridge. The famous harness that whirled her over the heads of the audience every night was not very sophisticated. A burly prop man, attached to one end of the harness, mounted a tall ladder with a rope connecting him to the tiny Sandy. When he jumped off the ladder, she "flew."

John Dyson and Bill Doyle left the department of Commerce for other pursuits. The new Commissioner of Commerce was William D. Hassett, Jr., a Buffalo businessman; the new Senior Deputy Commissioner was Natel Matschulat. Bill Hassett devoted his considerable skills and persuasive voice chiefly to the campaign for Economic Development that flourished during his tenure.

Natel, a petite blonde with one of the most brilliant marketing minds I have ever encountered, was determined to lead "I Love New York" to new heights. And she did. Natel and Marty Stern believed they could interest airlines in spending cooperative dollars behind running the Broadway show tours commercials, establishing special "I Love New York" fares, and filling seats during off-peak periods. At the outset, New York and the airlines split the television costs fifty-fifty. The program was immediately so successful that airlines began vying for the right to run the commercial. By the time Japan Airlines ran it in Tokyo, they were delighted to pay for the whole thing.

There were certain aspects of working for the state that took some adjusting for those of us more accustomed to the Procter & Gambles of the advertising world. For instance, all our Wells, Rich, Greene invoices were handled by a group of stern, apparently humorless chaps from a department called "Audit and Control."

One of my first debates with them took place over a beautiful magazine advertisement we had created to persuade tourists that New York State's fall foliage was just as beautiful as Vermont's, and a lot more accessible to many urban areas. The four-color photograph depicting the foliage was our proof, the reason to believe.

A few weeks later, I received word from Audit and Control that payment of the invoice for the advertisement was being withheld. "Why," the auditors asked, "was it necessary to spend so much extra money to produce this ad in *color?*"

I wrote back a long and reasonable explanation. More weeks passed. A second auditor wrote to say my letter was interesting, but were there any authorities on the subject of portraying autumn leaves in color as opposed to black and white?

I sighed, and sent them David Ogilvy's book, with a paper clip at the page on "story appeal in illustrations." They paid the bill.

It was the first of many encounters. Ultimately, I was able to convince the powers that be to arrange a face-to-face meeting with the Audit and Control folks. They discovered the people from Madison Avenue were not charlatans; we discovered the financial controllers were not simply dyspeptic. They needed to understand a little more about advertising; we gave them a basic course, and from that point on, finances ran smoothly.

In the copy of that same advertisement encouraging fall foliage tours, we offered a beautiful poster, suitable for framing, of drawings of twelve leaves native to New

York State. The cost was only a dollar, chiefly to cover postage and handling. More than twelve thousand people sent in their dollar for the poster, an amount which covered the cost of the printing and made a modest profit in the bargain. I received a verbal rap on the knuckles from the office of the attorney general. It seems it is illegal for the Department of Commerce to make money!

I was in Albany at least once a week, and the means of travel to and from the capital were capricious. Best of all, of course, was one of the state jets when the matter was top priority and involved the governor or the commissioner. There were always the boxy but comfortable planes of Command Airways. My favorite method, when time permitted, was taking the train, with its route right along the Hudson River all the way. It is one of the world's most beautiful rivers, and rivals the best the Rhine can offer.

Much of the time we drove, sometimes in state cars, sometimes in a car owned by one of the agency people. One lovely spring day, Dolores Zahn volunteered to be the driver. Marty Stern's niece was visiting from Germany, and Dolores offered to show her around Albany while we held our meetings. Dolores drives well but fast. Just short of Albany, a police car made us pull over. A young, pink-cheeked trooper wrote out the ticket.

"Oh, I'm so ashamed," Dolores said. "And me with my son a sergeant of police in Florida. I won't be able to face him."

"Jeez, lady," the young policeman said, "why didn't you tell me *before* I wrote the ticket?"

"I Love New York" was for me an example of what David Ogilvy called "seizing the moment." I caught the wave at just the right time, and had the good sense to ride it in. My direction of the campaign led to speaking engagements all over the country. College and university business classes, such as those at Yale, wanted to study the classic case history. Associations involved in tourism, like the Hotel Sales Management Association, wanted to create programs as successful as New York's.

I was even invited to visit Japan. One morning a telex arrived from the All-Japan Feminist Association in cooperation with the American Embassy. "Considering to invite you to speaking tour in Japan," the message began.

I telexed back immediately that I would be honored to accept.

The next day a second message came from Tokyo. "Considering, only considering," it went, and asked for further credentials. I was up against formidable competition. The year before, writer Adrienne Rich had been their speaker. I sent along my curriculum vitae and a copy of the Japanese edition of *How to Advertise*. The next telex from Japan confirmed dates.

Michael put me on the plane Thanksgiving morning. I read, ate, watched movies and slept, and arrived in Tokyo sixteen hours later, feeling wonderful. My hostess, feminist poet Ikuko Atsumi, not only met me at the airport, but graciously invited me to stay at her home in Tokyo, an honor not often extended by Japanese hosts. The house was Western in style, but one still took off one's shoes in the foyer and put on one of the many pairs of house slippers arrayed there. Further etiquette demanded that house slippers not be worn in the bathroom. There were special bathroom slippers for that, shared by the entire household.

I was indebted to a fellow American also staying at Ikuko's home, for a guide to Japanese good manners. "There's no shower," she alerted me. "Will you have trouble washing your hair?"

"No problem," I said. "My hair is so short I can soap and rinse right under the tap of the tub."

"Uh-uh," Diane Simpson warned. "The Japanese never but never use soap in the tub. It's for rinsing already clean, soap-free bodies." Diane taught me about the necessary gymnastics for shampoos.

The Japanese are the most caring hosts possible. The only mistake I made was in telling everyone in advance that I adore sashimi. So every single person who entertained me during the six days I spent there made it a point of honor to take me to a sashimi restaurant. Six days of nothing but raw fish can make even the most devout sashimi lover yearn for a hamburger. Well done.

I gave three speeches: two in Tokyo, one in Osaka, with a Japanese interpreter provided for each. There are two kinds of translation. Simultaneous translation, like that used by the United Nations, where the listeners follow through headphones. And sequential translation, the kind we used, whereby I'd say a sentence or two and the translator would render them into Japanese.

My first speech in Tokyo began with a rather nice joke. The interpreter translated. The audience roared. Later, an American woman who spoke fluent Japanese congratulated me on the speech. "I know you're doing it again in Osaka tomorrow," she said. "It's perfect, except for that opening joke."

"But it got a big laugh," I objected.

The American hesitated an instant. "Actually," she pointed out, "the interpreter said, 'Mrs. Maas has just told funny story which is impossible to translate. Please laugh.'"

I dropped the joke from my next speech.

Four of us boarded the famous "bullet" train from Tokyo to Osaka: Ikuko; advertising woman Terue Ohashi; Michiko Obiyashi, who had just returned from studying English in the United States and was assigned to me as personal guide; and myself. We bought "box lunches" that were works of art, and watched the countryside rush by. Kate had given me a furry little toy mascot, Colin James, as a good-luck token. He traveled in my handbag, and I held him up for a better view. The entire car chuckled.

After the speech in Osaka, we took a taxi to Kyoto for the treat of the visit, an overnight stay at a traditional Japanese inn. A long soak in a cedar-smelling hot tub, green tea, and to bed, dressed in soft cotton sleeping clothes, under warm, silky quilts.

The only "at liberty" day of the trip was the day in Kyoto. Michiko and Terue arranged for a Japanese tea ceremony in the morning, then Michiko took me on a tour of some of the old temples in the hills. It was full autumn in Japan, and hundreds of pilgrims kneeled in silence admiring "the crimson," the changing colors of one tree, or even one branch, framed in a doorway.

Back in Tokyo for my last day and my last speech. I bought presents for Kate and Jenny easily enough, but Michael wanted some of the renowned Japanese kitchen knives. Michiko steered me to Kiya, quintessential knife store. The more knives they showed me, the more I wanted to buy. Each was bigger and sharper than the last. Finally, I pointed to a really huge knife hanging on the wall. Nothing but the best for Michael, I figured. He'd really be able to fillet his bluefish in style. "That one."

Michiko and the sales clerk had a spirited discussion in Japanese. "Not possible," Michiko told me gently. "That is samurai sword." We settled for ordinary fillet knives.

Dentsu, the world's largest advertising agency, invited me to exchange views with their creative people. My escort, Shoji Tanaka, who had visited me in New York while he was researching his own book on American advertising, pointed out Dentsu's headquarters on the Ginza. At that time, Wells, Rich, Greene was the fourteenth-largest advertising agency in America, and we occupied three entire floors of the General Motors Building on Fifth Avenue. Tanaka San pointed out Dentsu's domain: two entire skyscrapers!

Dentsu, Tokyo, then employed five hundred copywriters. "How many of them are women?" I asked. "One." My hosts added that she was considered perhaps the best copywriter in all of Dentsu. A group of us went to lunch (sashimi, of course), then it was time for my final speech of the tour.

It was Standing Room Only in Gas Hall on the Ginza, as Tokyo's advertising community gathered to hear the "I Love New York" case history. I am almost never nervous making speeches; in fact, I love being on stage as much now as I did in my old Bucknell theater days. For some reason though, that day in Gas Hall my knees were knocking. It might have been that formidable professional audience. It might simply have been fatigue. The introduction was performed, and the audience applauded. On impulse, I took Kate's furry toy mascot, Colin James, up to the podium with me. "Good afternoon," I said. "I am very pleased to be here. And so is Colin James." He was a wonderful icebreaker. The audience immediately gave him a warm welcome, and I relaxed into my speech. I have hundreds of photos of my speaking tour in Japan, but none more charming than Colin James and I sharing the podium in Tokyo.

Japan is a marvelous country, especially for me. Everybody jogs, and hundreds of strangers greeted me with a smile and "Ohayo" as I ran every morning around the Olympic Stadium, not far from Ikuko's home. Most women in Japan are just about my height. For the first time in my life I rode the subways (daringly, with my destination, written in Japanese, pinned to my coat) without having to stand on tiptoe to reach the strap. Nowhere have strangers been kinder.

No wonder the Japanese create such brilliant advertising. They are competitive, determined, and compassionate, all qualities no creative person should be without.

I arrived home at 1155 Park Avenue at 11 A.M. the

following Friday morning and called Michael at his office. I remember sitting on the bed in my bathrobe, talking to him. "I'm just about to take a shower," I said. "I have a Bucknell board meeting at the Warwick Hotel at noon."

"You sound like you're talking through a muffler," Michael said. "Why don't you just go to bed."

"Go to bed?" I said huffily. "I feel just fine. Not a drop of jet lag." At ten that night, Michael peered down at me. "Want to get out of that bathrobe and into a nice fresh nightshirt?"

There was another personal bonus directly related to "I Love New York." In 1981, Women in Communications Inc. voted me the Matrix Award, their highest honor. Previous winners included historian Barbara Tuchman, Barbara Walters, Ada Louise Huxtable and advertising great Shirley Polykoff of "Does she or doesn't she?" fame. It was like entering the French Academy and taking a seat among the immortals.

Every year there are six winners, for the fields of journalism, broadcasting, advertising, public relations, magazines and writing. The bumper crop in 1981 included Letitia "Tish" Baldrige, who had been social secretary at the White House during the Kennedy years. Tish spent most of her preaward moments in the VIP suite trying to rid her dress of static cling. Other winners were Judy Daniels, then editor of *Savvy* magazine, and Pegeen Fitzgerald, of the long-running radio Fitzgeralds. Each of us was allotted two minutes for an acceptance comment. Pegeen said she couldn't wait to go home and tell Ed all the gossip, including the fact that Tish Baldrige had static cling. Pegeen went way over her two minutes, but she was so funny nobody counted. Judy Daniels railed against what she perceived to be the government's antifeminist stand. Tish Baldrige administered a ladylike scolding to Judy Daniels. Then I got up and thanked Michael Maas for making it all possible. There was loud applause. I could see that Michael was leading it.

"I Love New York" continued its momentum. The legislature continued to vote the tourism campaign an annual budget of ten million dollars, and the budget for Economic Development grew, too.

Bill Hassett left public life temporarily to devote more time to his family. His beautiful and talented assistant, Elaine Kerner, stayed on to become assistant to the new Commissioner of Commerce, George Dempster. George devoted most of his considerable energy and vision to Economic Development. During his tenure, the "Made in New York" campaign was created. Lyrics were written to the music of "I Love New York" and used for television and radio commercials. Print advertisements featured the "Made in New York" stamp. And thousands of New York State companies contacted the Department of Commerce to say they wanted to tie in with the program.

In 1980 and 1981, I was directing both the Tourism and Economic Development programs, and spending at least one day a week in Albany. Perhaps it was inevitable that I would wind up playing a role in the unpredictable life of Governor Hugh L. Carey.

Michael's brother, Peter, had long been a friend of Hugh Carey, and the governor was always cordial to me even though he didn't know me well. Our real friendship began one Friday in late September, 1980, when he called the agency to ask my help in a special project.

The governor had declared the second weekend in October a statewide "I Love New York" Fall Festival, and the main events were to take place in the huge Albany mall. He wanted to hold a reception at the Executive Mansion and turn its rather dreary second floor into a sort of club room that celebrated "Great Moments in New York State

Sports History." He asked me to help him find and frame those appropriate sports moments.

I had managed to get through four years of Bucknell without ever seeing a football game, and other sports are equally mysterious to me. I told the governor the project was right down my alley.

The biggest problem was time. The festival was only two weeks away. The second problem was sheer quantity, since the governor told me he wanted lots of photos. Hundreds of them, to fill the walls of the lobbylike space that separated the big bedrooms on the second floor.

The governor suggested that I come up and inspect the room. "How about tonight?" I asked, thinking about deadlines. "And suppose I bring Michael, for his architectural eye?" Hugh Carey was delighted. He was to make a dinner speech at the "21" Club that night, and asked if we would meet him there about 8:30 to fly with him to Albany on the state plane.

Michael and I had a lovely dinner at "21," as we always do. About 9:30, one of the governor's aides appeared to say the dinner event was running late. Why didn't we have a coffee and brandy; the governor would be along shortly. Michael and I obediently had a brandy and coffee. An hour passed. Michael had a second brandy and coffee. I wanted a bed. Finally, the agents came to collect us, we sped off to Butler Aviation, and boarded the jet for Albany. God knows what time we reached the Mansion.

Hugh Carey insisted on giving us a grand tour, more for Michael's benefit than mine. Here was the room Queen Elizabeth slept in while she was Princess Elizabeth. Here was the table Franklin D. Roosevelt used while he was governor of New York, with the marks of his wheel chair in its base. We staggered to bed about 4 A.M.

Like many great men (and women), Hugh Carey thrives on little sleep. He woke us cheerily at 9 A.M.

wearing his jogging clothes, informed us he'd already been for a run, and invited the "Imperial Architect" to inspect the picture gallery. Workmen were swarming over the area, sawing, painting, plastering. Michael emerged from the "Princess" bedroom in his Brooks Brothers red flannel nightshirt, armed with pad, pencil, and measuring tape. The workmen stopped in their tracks to watch this Ghost of Christmas Past. The pert Irish maid on duty that morning came upstairs to ask us what we would like for breakfast. "Phyllis," Michael said, "I would give my life for a beer."

Phyllis behaved as if unshaven men in long red nighties were part of any normal morning at the Mansion. She kept Michael supplied with beer and scrambled eggs, served on a sawhorse, all morning.

Michael and the governor had a difference of opinion as to the right size of the photos. The governor, as noted, wanted lots of little ones. "Governor," Michael objected, "this is majestic space. You approach it up a big formal stairway. The ceilings are immense. You need a dozen, perhaps eighteen big, dramatic photos, in scale with the room." Hugh Carey agreed, and the hunt for the pictures was on.

Dolores, thank goodness, is a sports buff. She can also charm the birds out of the trees. So she spent the next week calling the wire services, magazine archives and photo collections. Permission to reproduce a negative can cost thousands of dollars, so Dolores pleaded the cause of the state and its great gallery. Among the famous photos we collected were O. J. Simpson, Mickey Mantle, Joe Namath, and my own favorite, the moment our ice hockey team won the 1980 Olympic games.

Michael "loaned" me his director of graphics, Terry Colbert, to hang the show. We drove to Albany the Friday morning of the festival weekend, with a station wagon full of photos, and worked against the clock to get the exhibit on the walls before the reception began at 6 P.M. When the governor arrived to inspect the room, I was in jeans and a T-shirt, filthy from head to foot. "You are the perfect role model for women advertising executives," he teased.

The Fall Festival was a roaring success. Crowds began gathering at dawn on Saturday. Sesame Street's Big Bird was one of the first acts, followed by Steve Karmen conducting the New York State Orchestra in "I Love New York," Kitty Carlisle Hart and Hugh Carey singing a medley, and Leonard Bernstein reminiscing. By nightfall, a crowd of ninety thousand people jammed the mall to hear rock group The Manhattans and watch fireworks.

At dinner that night in the Mansion, not a single guest was allowed to miss the sports display on the second floor. I gather that one of the first actions of Matilda Cuomo when she became First Lady was to take it all down. Alas.

Michael was not able to come to Albany for the weekend, so I invited Natel Matschulat as my "date." The governor came over to the table where my dinner partner was the witty Brother Driscoll, president of Iona College. "Michael isn't here?" the governor asked, his eyebrows raised. "Doesn't he know a gubernatorial invitation takes precedence over anything else? Bad cess to his impudence. Where is he?"

I explained that Michael was playing golf at Pine Valley, that mecca for golfers. Hugh Carey is a man who has his priorities in perfect order at all times. "Good for Mike," he said. "Wish I were with him."

A few weeks later I was back in Albany to supervise the taking of a historic photo. The governor, together with the majority *and* minority leaders of the state assembly and senate, had agreed to pose together for one of our Economic Development advertisements, shaking hands over the passage of a new probusiness bill. At the appointed hour, one of the leaders was missing. Word came down that he insisted on a change in the copy before he would pose. The other four men, their press aides, and my client would all have to approve the revision. We postponed the shoot.

Governor Carey took pity on my plight, and invited me to the Mansion for dinner. Over a glass of New York State wine, he talked to me about his happy marriage, his twelve children, his loneliness since the death of his wife some years earlier, and the difficulties of being a single parent. "People think I have a lot of fun being a bachelor," he confided. "They think I love all this freedom. But I'm a one-woman man, and I'm looking for one woman to settle down with."

In January, the day he attended the Reagan inauguration in Washington, the governor found her. She was Evangeline Gouletas, known as Engie, one of the three founders, with her brothers Nicholas and Victor, of American Invsco, a Chicago-based real-estate firm.

"I want you and Michael to meet Engie," the governor said. "Why don't the four of us go to mass next Sunday, then on to brunch." From that point on, Engie, the governor, Michael, and I were together for lots of brunches and lots of evenings. Sometimes we'd be at official dinners or grand restaurants, more often at the informal little places the governor prefers. Engie introduced us to one or two Greek after-dinner spots, where we listened to bouzouki music and watched men perform an acrobatic dance. The governor was pretty good at learning the dance; Michael never let me cajole him onto the dance floor. He does a basic fox trot to just about any music, from a waltz to a tango, but he wasn't about to take on bouzouki.

As the romance progressed, I became the governor's confidante. These were heady days. Often, I'd be in the midst of a meeting with a clutch of deputy commissioners discussing some forthcoming ad, when the telephone would ring. "The governor is calling for Mrs. Maas," somebody would announce. The room always fell silent.

"I think Engie had a good time last evening, don't you?" the governor would ask.

"I certainly do, sir," I would reply solemnly.

All eyes in the room were on me. Were we discussing the state budget? The next election?

"Any suggestions about next steps?"

"Well, sir, that will take a little strategic thinking." I loved every minute of it.

In March, Michael and I flew to Chicago to join the governor, Engie, and Engie's family and friends to celebrate her "Name's Day." For Greeks, one's Name's Day (the day of the saint after whom you are named) is far more important than a birthday. Hugh Carey gave Engie a ring that was, coincidentally, almost identical to the one that Prince Charles gave Lady Diana at about the same time. The governor and Engie both declared it a "friendship ring," but those of us close to them guessed it meant something more.

On a Sunday late in March, the governor invited Michael and me to meet with him and Engie at her New York pied-à-terre for a "serious little talk." I had a hunch they might be planning a June wedding.

"We've decided to get married," they told us. We all hugged and kissed.

"On Hugh's birthday," Engie added. "And, most important of all, we want someone who loves us and is close to us to run the wedding. Jane, will you do it for us?"

"I've never run a wedding," I stammered. "Not even my own." The thought going through my mind was, "I don't do windows. I don't do weddings. I'm in advertising."

"I think you can't refuse," Michael said quietly.

"If you really, really want me to, of course I will," I

agreed. "And I'm flattered you've asked me. What's the date?"

"My birthday," the governor answered. "Two weeks from yesterday."

Hours later, it hit me. We had only thirteen days to prepare for all the pomp and circumstance of a state wedding.

First thing next morning I asked Mary Lawrence and Fred Jacobs for a leave of absence without pay, so there would be no conflict with Wells, Rich, Greene and the New York State account. Next was a call to Tish Baldrige to ask her professional advice on the protocol for a wedding of this magnitude.

Tish was wonderfully calm. She had recently written the new edition of *The Amy Vanderbilt Book of Etiquette,* and knew the answers to every question.

"The first thing to do is order the invitations from Tiffany's," Tish mused. "Should we use the gubernatorial seal? Oh yes, I think so. Now, engraving will take at least two weeks, and calligraphy another five days. When is the wedding?"

"A week from Saturday," I said.

Tish reeled. "How will we ever get the invitations out in time?"

I had already discussed this issue with the bride. "Mailgrams."

Tish was stricken, but recovered. "Sometimes the finer points of etiquette must bow to larger concerns," she agreed. "But there are some dictates we simply must follow. The governor is a widower; Mrs. Gouletas is a widow. Since this is a second marriage for both, the wedding ceremony must be small. Only one attendant for each. Immediate family only."

I passed this information along to Engie, who smiled a

small, quiet smile. "With one Greek family and one Irish family, the immediate family is very, very large."

Tish also suggested that an engagement photo would be appropriate, and Engie agreed. Through Tish, we were able to book the great fashion photographer Horst, on short notice. Engie, Tish, and I waited in a studio for the arrival of the groom. A siren sounded in the distance, then grew louder. It was obviously coming our way. "Here comes Hugh," Engie said.

"How wonderful to know your true love cometh when you hear a siren," Tish said. The governor raced up the studio steps and hugged Engie for a long minute. They both looked tense. Could they have a few moments alone together before the photo session began? Of course they could.

Later, they told me the news. Engie's husband was not dead at all. He was alive, living in California. Shortly, two other ex-husbands were revealed. For all of us who loved Engie and the governor, the days were a nightmare. For them, it must have been sheer hell.

Let me set the record straight. Evangeline Gouletas-Carey is an extraordinary woman who has been unfairly maligned by the press. She is a very private person, whose only thought was to protect her daughter, Maria, and her two young grandchildren from malicious publicity. Nothing in Engie's entire life had prepared her for the prying and poking of journalists.

In his bestselling book, *Mayor,* Ed Koch speaks of his affection for Engie Carey, calling her sensitive, shy, a superb businesswoman, and a great comfort to Hugh Carey. "I like her," he says simply.

Engie and Hugh did not let the ugly gossip affect the final days of their courtship. As the great day approached, we had a dozen volunteers on duty almost around the clock at "Wedding Central," as we dubbed the family offices assigned to the planning staff. Western

Union assigned us a special staffer just to help with the tons of mailgram invitations and acceptances to and from all parts of the world.

Designer George Stavropoulos and his seamstresses worked night and day. George was designing not only Engie's wedding gown and the dress she would wear at the banquet the evening of the wedding, but also the gowns for all the bridesmaids. Generous Engie included not only her own daughter, but all the governor's daughters as well. There are five of them, so George was busy. "Every time I look up, here comes another bridesmaid," he moaned to me over the phone. (My biggest role of the entire wedding, really, was listening patiently to moans.)

The governor's security people moaned. There were going to be twice as many wedding guests as we anticipated, and to top off their concerns, the governor and Engie planned to ride from the church to the reception in an open car. Engie said, "The governor belongs to the people. We invite the entire city of New York to be part of the wedding." Security moaned louder.

The St. Regis was selected as site for the reception, and with good reason. Hugh Carey's son, Chris, was banquet manager. Wonderful as that hotel is, it had no one public room large enough for our Royal Wedding. As we made our tour of inspection, the dismal truth began to dawn on me. "Well," I said, "let's face it. We're going to have to throw *two* receptions, one on the second floor, one on the St. Regis roof." It was my turn to moan. We needed two wedding cakes, two state swords to cut them, two dance bands, two official pipers, and double security guards.

Tish Baldrige taught us all how to run the perfect receiving line with a minimum of delays. There is one "pusher" and one "puller." The "pusher" urges guests into the line, while the "puller" literally tugs them by the hand out of it, breaking up any cozy little chats.

April 11 dawned sunny and warm. The immense

Greek Orthodox Church was packed. Engie floated down the aisle, with her six bridesmaids, preceded by her granddaughter as flower girl. The governor had three best men, Nicholas Gouletas, his brother Edward Carey, and his good friend Nick Brady. The seven Carey sons were ushers. The immediate family was large, as predicted.

At the St. Regis, the two-tiered reception went off without a flaw. At 4 P.M. I turned to Michael. "Nobody's been trampled to death," I said. "I think it's a success."

I came home and told Kate and Jenny they would simply have to elope. I don't do windows. And from now on, I don't do weddings. But I wouldn't have missed it for all the rice in China.

Wild Animals I Have Known

*T*here is a rule in the world
of television commercials. "If it involves animals, double
the price." The same rule holds true for fractious celebrities, and babies. I have not yet been involved with babies,
and all the celebrities I have worked with were lambs, but
the animals were sometimes more than an animal act.

My first experience was working with the doves in the
Dove-for-Dishes campaign. Each commercial began with
a dove flying across the screen and into somebody's window, while a startled onlooker exclaimed, "I could have
sworn I saw a dove fly into Susie Smith's window!"

The birds were put through their paces by the same
man who trained the birds for Alfred Hitchcock's film of
the same name. Some days our doves sailed gallantly into
the window for take after take. Some days they sulked.

When they didn't perform on cue, a prop man would
tie string to their feet and yank them through the window. The doves would screech and spread their wings in
protest, giving us some of our most dramatic footage.
The string was invisible on film, and the ASPCA never
showed up at the studio, so nobody ever complained. Except the doves.

Another hazard of working with birds came when they
got away from their trainer and nested in the topmost

rafters of the studio. Wardrobe mistresses had to hold umbrellas (high enough to be out of camera range) over the actors to protect them from unseemly accidents that could delay filming. The rest of us just took cover.

My Copy Group head, Gene Grayson, had a cute idea for advertising Milky Way candy bars during the summer months, when many people like to freeze them. He wanted to have a polar bear take a Milky Way out of an ice container, eat the bar and then say, through the voice of an actor, "I'm a bear for frozen Milky Ways."

The client loved the storyboard, and gave the agency an immediate go-ahead. Jack Silverman, then head of Broadcast Production, became part of the team. He quickly discovered the first problem. Polar bears are notorious for their ugly dispositions; they are perhaps the least tractable and trainable of animals. Scouts scoured the world, and we finally received the news that one fairly docile polar bear existed. She was in the zoo at Mexico City.

Grayson and Silverman took the precaution of having three special ice containers constructed for the commercial before they left New York, not knowing what resources they might find in Mexico. Each had a carefully silk-screened picture of the Milky Way bar on the lid.

In Mexico City, the bear's keeper suggested that the surest way to lure the bear toward the chest was to fill the inside with lots of fish oil, the smellier the better, in addition to the Milky Way bars. The camera rolled, the polar bear hurried toward the luscious smell inside the chest, and fiddled for several moments with the cover.

Nobody had considered that polar bears are not all that adept in opening ice chests. The polar bear, a svelte young female weighing over nine hundred pounds, lost patience, reared on her hind legs, and smashed the chest to smithereens. One down, two to go.

Cue the second chest, cue the codfish oil, cue the bear.

The bear smashed the second chest, too, only this time she smashed it faster, having learned from experience. With only one chest left to go, Silverman had a prop man with a fishing rod hang over the bear pit. As the bear approached the chest, and seemed to reach for it, the prop man jerked the rod and the lid flew open. The bear appeared on film to be going bonkers over Milky Ways.

Recalls Grayson, "Do you have any idea how strong codfish oil smells? Combined with the smell of polar bear, it's even more pungent. Toss in two days of shooting in heat over one hundred degrees. Jack Silverman and I had to throw away all our clothes, but people still avoided us for weeks."

One of the most famous use of animals on television was Ogilvy & Mather's charging herd of bulls for Merrill Lynch. The first commercial was filmed on location in Mexico. Why Mexico? Recalls copywriter Bruce Silverman, now executive creative director of BBDO/West: "The art director and I were both kids from Brooklyn. All we knew about bulls was what we saw on bullfighting posters. So the art director drew a herd of black bulls. It turned out the only place you can find those bulls is Mexico. So we went to Mexico.

"We hired about a thousand bulls, twenty Mexican cowboys, and a crew from New York. Nobody remembered to bring along an interpreter. I don't know what language the bulls spoke, but we sure couldn't communicate with the cowboys. So there we were, in the middle of the Mexican desert, living in trailers for about two weeks, out of communication with the rest of the world."

The storyboard began with just a speck of dust on the horizon. The speck grew and grew in size until the viewer saw an entire herd of bulls charging directly at the camera, and then—seemingly—passing right over it. How was that incredible effect achieved?

It was, in fact, no effect at all. The crew dug a big fox-hole, which could be covered with a steel plate. The cameraman, copywriter, art director, and producer all huddled in the trench as the herd charged toward them. Just before the bulls reached the foxhole, they would slam the steel hatch and keep shooting upward, periscope style.

"We sweated a lot and prayed a lot, especially when the bulls were going over," Silverman adds. "The only one smart enough to stay out of the foxhole was the client."

The creative team arrived back in New York, sun-poisoned but triumphant, to learn that the agency had been trying frantically to locate them and tell them for God's sake to stop shooting. The client had canceled the commercial!

The original storyboard did not contain the words that finally were heard on television. It called for the speck of dust to turn into the herd of bulls and then have the announcer declare, "At Merrill Lynch, we spot the trends."

A terrible glitch developed. Some Iago whispered into the ear of the Merrill Lynch advertising manager, "Merrill Lynch spots the trends! What kind of slogan is that? I'd fire any broker who *didn't* spot the trends." The advertising manager reported his grave second thoughts about the line. Now the agency sat with a small fortune invested in bulls charging at the camera, and no reason to use them. Almost every writer in the place was asked to work on the problem.

Copywriter Roger Butler came up with the line "Merrill Lynch is bullish on America." The client approved it. The commercial went on the air. Only a few nights later, President Nixon declared in a nationally televised speech that just like Merrill Lynch, he too was bullish on America. The slogan was soon on every tongue.

Clearly, a second commercial needed to be filmed before the first one suffered "wear out." We had been taken to task in the press for filming our "bullish on America" commercial in Mexico, so this time we were careful to choose a location in California. We used a different strain of bull, but everyone expected they would perform as well as their Mexican cousins.

Copywriter Peter Hochstein (one of the funniest writers in our business), who was there, recalls: "A bull is an ornery, lazy, vicious animal with all the eagerness to please of an enraged tarantula, and just enough imagination to make your life miserable.

"The storyboard looked easy enough, though. It called for a herd of bulls to stampede along a beach while a voice-over announcer recited a tone poem to the effect that Merrill Lynch was bullish on America.

"But a bull will not necessarily run where you want it to run, and will not run at all unless you persuade it that there is good and verifiable reason for total panic. So a team of eleven rodeo cowboys were hired to ride horseback behind the bulls, shouting, howling, cracking whips and firing shotguns in the air, while seven camera crews, including one in a hovering helicopter, filmed whatever might occur.

"You'd think that blood-curdling yells, whip cracks and gun shots would be enough to panic *any* creature, but after four or five takes, the bulls got the idea that this was just some advertising routine, and they figured the hell with it. When the commotion began on the sixth take, some of the bulls meandered down to the water's edge to take an experimental chaw of seaweed, one of them charged the director with intent to maim or kill, two of them began putting on an X-rated performance, and the rest just stood around enjoying the sight of all those advertising people nervously tearing their hair out.

"By the seventh take, two bulls decided to go AWOL and take a swim in the Pacific Ocean. We had been assured by the chief wrangler that it is against the nature of a bull to step in water deeper than its own hoof, but these bulls evidently weren't playing by the rules of nature.

"Within seconds, the bulls were in the Pacific literally up to their necks, waves were breaking over their heads, and, now in a real panic, they were struggling out to sea instead of turning back and heading for shore.

"Our wranglers were not optimistic. 'You can forget them two suckers,' one mourned. 'You cain't herd 'em back to shore because the horses won't go into surf that deep, and you cain't call 'em back because they're too ignorant to listen. You're looking at about a ton of perfectly good beef about to turn itself into s! .rk food.'

"We remembered how the press had reported the filming in Mexico as a scandal. The last thing we needed now were stories that Ogilvy & Mather and Merrill Lynch had wantonly drowned innocent bulls.

"Suddenly the director got an idea. He picked up the walkie talkie and instructed the helicopter pilot to fly over the ocean above the bulls, and then charge at them head on.

"It worked. The roaring helicopter swooped out of the sky at the bulls. The terrified bulls bellowed, turned away from the menacing machine, and swam to dry land.

"This not only saved the bulls, it gave us a technique that saved the entire production. We immediately rented a second helicopter, and used it to start a panic-motivated stampede every time the director called for action. It never failed to work, and we got over forty marvelous takes before we called it a wrap."

The bull who performed the "bull in a china shop" commercial for Merrill Lynch was specially trained by going through a routine in a maze made of crates and hay bales to simulate what he eventually would face on the set of the commercial. On the day of filming, "Merrill" navigated the china shop so deftly that he didn't break a single piece. It was the set designer who nervously dropped and broke a candelabra worth $3,500.

My old friend Brendan Kelley created one of the most ambitious animal commercials ever filmed, featuring a herd of elephants. The client was Elephant Premium Floppy Discs, which uses the slogan "Elephants Never Forget." To introduce a new line of discs aimed at the business market, Kelley and his creative team devised a storyboard with elephants charging Wall Street.

The logo for Elephant Floppy Discs portrays an African elephant, with tusks and big floppy ears. Elephant trainers advised that African elephants are wild and hard to work with, and suggested the more placid Asian elephant. Unfortunately, Asian elephants have small ears and no tusks, so a special-effects man was called in to add "falsies" to their ears and affix fake tusks.

The creative folks and the production company next learned from the trainers that, since elephants are very social animals, they must get acquainted with each other before they can work together. So the herd was taken off to a ranch in New Jersey to socialize for two days before the shoot. Rick Levine Productions called it "The Elephant Cocktail Party."

The commercial was filmed on a Sunday, and went like clockwork. By Monday morning, the only hint on Wall Street that a herd of elephants had just charged through were dumpsters of elephant dung.

The Maas family has had our own share of animals including Leo (a psychotic Abyssinian cat); Walter (a manic-depressive cat who hurled himself from a window; we remember him as "Walter the Flyer"); gerbils (we began with a mommy and a daddy, but after they had a brood of twelve we had to pay the pet store to take them back); and one parrot, known as Polly. Jenny insisted on taking Polly to her first-grade class for Show and Tell one blustery December day, despite my protests. Next day, we woke to find Polly cold, feet up in her cage. Michael summoned the apartment super, and handed Polly over, cage and all. He explained to Jenny, "Polly would have wanted to go down with her ship."

We had a mouse for a while, too, called Georgette. Michael and I arrived in Westhampton one Friday afternoon in summer to find Kate, Jenny, and our housekeeper all in tears. Georgette seemed to have the flu, and would daddy rush her to the vet. We called for an appointment, and were asked rather sharply by the nurse if this were a *pet* mouse. Mich?el left for the animal hospital, with Georgette cradled in his hand for warmth.

In the waiting room, he encountered one of his golfing buddies, holding the leash of a fierce-looking Doberman. "Hey, Mike," he asked, "what kind of pet do you have?"

Michael silently opened his hand and revealed Georgette.

My favorite animal was Mr. Mickles, the only truly charming turtle I've ever met. He was a little green turtle, the kind you buy in a dime store, whose life expectancy is usually measured by months. Mr. Mickles lived for eight or nine years.

Toward the end of his life, he was ailing and refusing to eat. Kate and I bundled him up in cotton, put him in a jewelry box and headed for the only veterinarian in New York I could find who specialized in turtles. We hailed a cab. "Central Park West and 85th Street and step on it," I told the driver. "We have a very sick turtle here." He drove as though pursued by the hounds of hell.

The vet told us to feed Mr. Mickles delicacies and not to let him get cold. He recovered his appetite, all right, only to succumb soon afterward. We placed his aquarium on top of a radiator, and he died of accidental poaching. I suppose it's rather a nice way to go, like drifting off in a hot tub.

We wanted to give him proper burial in the "pet bury-
ing ground" in our back garden in Westhampton. So,
while waiting for the ground to thaw, I put him in a Baggie in the freezer. A friend went for ice cubes one evening, and her shriek indicated that she had come upon
Mr. Mickles.

Michael and I debated constantly about whether or not
to buy a dog. Soon after Kate was born, I made my argument on behalf of a puppy. "You had a dog when you
were a little boy," I said, "and I had a dog when I was a
little girl. Kate should have a dog, too."

"A dog in a New York apartment?" Michael replied.
"No way."

After Jenny was born four years later, I stepped up my
pleas. "The children shouldn't grow up without a dog."

"I'd end up walking it in the morning, I'd end up walking it in the evening," Michael said. "As long as we live in
an apartment, no dog."

About two years after Jenny's arrival, I said to Michael,
"What would you think about having a third child?"

Michael said, "How about a poodle?"

We acquired Mulligan, a look-alike for Snoopy, but a
dog of little brain. Michael did indeed walk him morning
and evening, and was the only one who mourned his loss
when we sent him, still not housebroken, to live with my
sister in the suburbs.

Dogs we used in commercials were a lot smarter. Usually. Once we were filming a commercial for a new General Foods dog food, using Arlene Francis as the
spokeswoman and a beautiful golden retriever as the
eater. First, since the commercial implied that the dog belonged to Arlene Francis, the dog indeed had to become
her dog. The creative team, which included vice president
and creative director Bruce Stauderman, who now heads
his own agency in Denver, convinced Ms. Francis's house-

hold staff that having a golden retriever around the house would be a joy and a pleasure.

A specialist in golden retrievers warned that these dogs could be delicate. If the campaign succeeded and we wanted to film more commercials over the next two or three years showing the young retriever growing up and thriving on the dog food, we had better have three identical dogs as fail-safe.

Back to Ms. Francis's household staff to convince them of the joy of owning not one golden retriever, but three. Mission accomplished, we turned to filming. The high moment of the commercial was to occur when the star retriever stood on his hind legs to be petted by Arlene Francis, then dropped down to eat the food. The dog stood, but he wouldn't drop.

The trainer volunteered a solution. He would stand behind Arlene Francis where he couldn't be seen, and hold one of the dog's paws. On cue, he would drop the dog's paw, and the dog would automatically go down on all fours. It worked, and the commercial was successfully completed, edited, and approved by the client, who watched it carefully on a moviola. The day before it was to go on air, the agency and client gathered for a party, and a showing of the commercial on a huge screen.

There stood Arlene Francis in an attractive gown. Her hand and arm reaching out so lovingly to the dog were burly and covered with dark hair. Too late. We went on air with the commercial, but nobody ever complained, not even Arlene Francis.

Another dog-loving celebrity who agreed to appear in a commercial for a different General Foods dog food was Doris Day, who owned nine or ten dogs, and cared deeply about their well-being. Only two days before the commercial was to be filmed, Jack Silverman received a call from Ms. Day's secretary, informing him that she would be unable to do the commercial after all.

Silverman was aghast. "Why not?" he asked. "What's the matter."

The secretary told him that Ms. Day had been eating the dog food, and did not like its taste.

"How do the dogs like it?" Silverman inquired.

It turned out that the dogs liked it just fine, and filming proceeded on schedule.

Here at Muller Jordan Weiss, we have only one account that needs animals, Goff cat food. When we produced our first commercial for them, we used animation. It wouldn't surprise me at all, though, to have a client turn up needing television commercials for anything from Crocodile Crayons to Cobra perfume. And somewhere there will be a creative team zany enough to come up with an idea, and a director crazy enough to film it.

Handmaiden to the Queen

Whenever I happen to mention that for seven months I ran my own agency, strangers look at me with respect. When I tell them the firm opened its doors with Leona Helmsley as its first and only client, their expressions change to amazement.

One question always follows. "What is Leona Helmsley really like?" That's a tough one, but let me try to answer it. She is everything you think she is from reading about her in her advertisements. And more.

Leona and I met for the first time at one of her fabled "I'm Just Wild About Harry" parties, held every year to celebrate Harry Helmsley's birthday. Leona, dressed in a golden gown, stood beside her six-foot-three-inch husband, greeting their guests. We all wore buttons that proclaimed I'M JUST WILD ABOUT HARRY. Harry wore the biggest button of all. It said I'M HARRY.

Every woman in the room wore a sweeping ballgown except me. I wore my best bib and tucker, a black velvet tuxedo. Once Leona knew me well enough to be candid, which took about two weeks, she told me what she thought about my attire. "You looked like a dyke, sweetheart."

Michael and I were invited to this special party through the good offices of Hugh Carey. The evening was to mark Evangeline Gouletas's introduction to New York society, and the governor told Leona that Engie might be more comfortable if a few people she already knew were there. An invitation was delivered to me by hand within hours.

Michael and I met the governor and Engie, and drove to the Park Lane (a Helmsley hotel of course), where Harry and Leona have a duplex apartment at the summit. Guests entered on the first of the two floors, then climbed a flight of stairs to the top floor, passed the big swimming pool, and entered the "den," where party regulars told us the real action was.

Watch David Susskind help himself to caviar from a container that appears to have the dimensions of a punchbowl. Michael tastes and approves. "Beluga." See the governors of New York and New Jersey confer, laughing. Note the flurry when Gregory Peck arrives. Another flurry when Mrs. Peck enters, and the women observe she is as lovely as reputed.

The beautiful and the famous have light chitchat. Kitty Carlisle Hart is talking with old friends author and editor Phyllis Cerf Wagner and her husband, Bob, former mayor of New York. Look around the packed room and you might spot a Rockefeller or two, Sonny Werblin, Douglas Fairbanks, Jr., Leon Hess, Walter Hoving, David Mahoney, Mike Wallace, Dan Rather, Gerry Tsai—all Helmsley friends.

After we have eaten and drunk our fill of caviar and champagne, the party moves down to the dining room of the Park Lane, closed to the public for the evening. All the guests are seated as the orchestra strikes up "I'm Just Wild About Harry" and our hosts enter. We all leap to our feet and applaud as Leona and Harry make their royal progress across the ballroom, Leona waving to the crowd, tossing imaginary bouquets to favorites. Balloons rain down on the dance floor. The birthday couple begins to dance, and it is obvious to everyone that they are having a simply marvelous time.

"The first time I ever danced with Harry, I knew we were right for each other," Leona told me weeks later. "I just fit into his arms." The Helmsleys are beautiful dancers, and they love to dance, especially with each other. They are almost always the first people on the dance floor when the orchestra starts up. Phyllis Wagner believes the Helmsleys help make any ordinary black-tie dinner a success. "They dance, so everybody dances. They make it fun."

My dinner partner, John Mazzola, then director of Lincoln Center, joined me in playing "Isn't that so-and-so?" as we looked around the celebrity-studded room. "Isn't it a shame that nobody who's really anybody comes to these parties?" he observed dryly.

At departure time, all the guests receive "Goody Bags," like the ones given out at children's parties. We are leaving a tad early, as the governor has a meeting in Albany at dawn, and the bags are not quite ready for distribution. "Never mind," I tell an attendant. "I don't need one."

"Oh no," she answers with a frightened look, "Mrs. Helmsley would be *very* angry." She puts the favors in little bags and gives one to each of us. One gift is a tiny music box that plays "I'm Just Wild About Harry."

"I wonder how much that party cost," I muse to Michael as we get into bed.

"It's like owning a yacht," Michael yawns. "If you have to ask, you can't afford it. Go to sleep."

I go to sleep, and no wild dream alerts me to the fact that for the next seven months I will be handmaiden to the Queen.

You've seen the advertisements for the Helmsley Palace: "The only hotel in the world where The Queen stands guard," with photos of Leona peering into the soup kettles, and supervising the flower arrangements. You've seen the advertisements for the Park Lane that show Leona writing letters in response to satisfied guests who thank the staff for retrieving a jewel lost in the thick carpet, obtaining a black bow tie at a moment's notice, or remembering a guest's favorite room. You've seen the advertisements for the Harley Hotel featuring Leona vowing that she can't stand skimpy bath towels, closet hangers that won't detach, or bathrooms without makeup mirrors. I didn't do those advertisements. They are the work of Beber, Silverstein & Partners, an agency Leona hired shortly after she and I parted ways. Leona was looking for an agency at the time she met me because she had just fired her previous agency, Beber, Silverstein.

My old friend Bill Dowling, an expert in hotel marketing and advertising, was directing the marketing for the Helmsley hotels in New York City and the twenty-odd hotels in the Harley chain nationwide. Bill was beside himself. It was late April, he was facing closing dates for important advertisements in early summer magazines, and he had no advertising.

"I've brought in other agencies. Mrs. Helmsley doesn't like them. I've brought in free-lancers. Mrs. Helmsley doesn't like them. If we don't get some ads on summer hotel packages, the occupancy will go down, and she'll have my head."

Bill told me Leona Helmsley knew I was in advertising and liked what she heard about me. Would I do some speculative advertisements to help him out of his dilemma? I agreed, on the condition that I could meet with Leona first to hear her thoughts about the hotels.

We met at the Park Lane for lunch. Leona swept toward the dining room with Bill Dowling and me in her wake. She stopped short and beckoned to a staffer stationed near the door. "You. Yes, you with the dirty fingernails. Come here."

The little man recoiled. Leona looked down in fury.
"Get those fingernails clean or don't come back tomorrow." She started away, then turned back. "I'll be here to check on you."

Greeting the maître d' in the dining room, Leona turned from tigress to pussycat. No one I have ever met is more gracious than Leona at her most gracious. I was charmed. All over the dining room, heads turned as guests realized who had just entered. *They* were charmed. Waiters and busboys snapped to attention. I thought most of the staff looked scared to death. Later I learned they were.

"Call her Mrs. Helmsley," Bill had warned me earlier. "She prefers to be formal."

"Have the tuna-fish salad," Leona urged me. "It's my own recipe. Low in calories, low in cholesterol. I invented it for my Harry, and I make them have it on the menu here every day."

Ordering anything else seemed inexcusable. "I'll have the tuna, Mrs. Helmsley," I said.

"Call me Leona, sweetheart."

Bill Dowling winced. "Jane wanted to hear your ideas about advertising, Mrs. Helmsley."

"Fine," she said. Bill winced again.

Only four days later, we were back in the Park Lane for tea, as Leona looked at rough layouts and sample copy for advertising campaigns. One campaign used the hotels as "heroes" of the advertisements. My experience working with hotel marketers for "I Love New York" had shown that people want to know what a hotel looks like, especially if it's a new one. The Harley, on 42nd Street, had just opened, and everybody wanted to see the exterior of the Helmsley Palace, since its façade was the famous old Villard House.

However, Leona's discussion with me had indicated that she was vitally involved in every aspect of the hotels, so, just to be on the safe side, the art director and I worked up one campaign featuring *her*. That was the one she preferred.

"I don't like being in the advertising. It's a security risk for me. I'm too busy to waste my time having photographs taken. My Harry doesn't like me doing it. But what can I do? If it's good for the hotels, I have to make the sacrifice."

Harry Helmsley arrived to collect his wife. Leona showed him the advertising. "Don't you love it, Harry?" She brightened with a sudden idea. "Why don't we set Jane up as an advertising agency? We can give her space in the Graybar Building (a Helmsley-Spear property) right away." Harry agreed. He didn't seem to regard setting up an advertising agency as much of a big deal.

Leona turned to me. "Do a good job for us, sweetheart, and I'll help you get lots of other clients. You can be a big, successful agency."

Like any red-blooded, independent-minded executive, I went home and asked Michael. "What do you think, hon?"

"As long as you have me and three square meals a day, what do you have to lose?" Michael said.

So I said yes. I didn't check with anybody about what Leona was like to work with or speak to her previous agency. Probably no man would have made such a precipitous decision. He would have checked out his Old Boy Network. Women still don't have a good Old-Girl Old-Boy Network. We're working on it, but we're not there yet.

Fred Papert, an old friend and former president of Papert, Koenig, Lois, the first advertising agency to go public, heard my news. "Is it true Leona Helmsley is your only client?" he asked.

"True," I said.

"Do you know anything about her?"

"Just that she's a doll."

Fred rolled his eyes. "Get some more clients."

Harry Helmsley and I signed the contract two days later. Dolores laughed as I left the General Motors building for that historic meeting. My hands were so cold with anxiety I couldn't activate the heat-sensitive elevator button. "Take me along with you," Dolores sang, knowing she didn't need to plead.

Leona pronounced the benediction after the contract was signed. "Never agree with me if you don't mean it, never 'yes' me, never lie to me, and we'll have a wonderful relationship."

The honeymoon was on. Norman Zahn moved Dolores and me into our "temporary" space in the Graybar Building. We would remain there for the entire seven months. It was one long, narrow room, divided by plastic partitions into work areas just big enough to squeeze in the five hotel reservation clerks who used to inhabit it.

The view from our barred and grilled window was of the air-conditioning ducts of the Hyatt Hotel. The whole space was about half the size and half the brightness of my park-view office at Wells, Rich, Greene. I thought it was heaven! Michael again loaned me his director of graphics, Terry Colbert, who designed a JANE MAAS, INC. plaque for the door and ordered stationery. Dolores rented an electric typewriter, and found an answering service. Art director George Stewart soon joined us as a vice president, followed by Dee Jackson, traffic director. We were official.

My friends at Wells threw a goodbye party for Dolores and me, and Mary wished me good luck with a hug. "I'm sad that you are leaving, and I hope you know we want you to come back if you ever decide to stop being entrepreneurial. But how could I, who started my own agency, do anything but wish you luck in starting yours."

Michael invited Leona and Harry and their good

friends Phyllis and Bob Wagner to dinner to celebrate the opening of Jane Maas, Inc. Leona was seated at Michael's right, and I noticed she was chatting vivaciously. Later he reported part of the conversation.

"You have magnificent eyebrows, Michael."

"I know."

"Look at me when I'm talking to you."

"When I talk to you, I will. Right now I'm listening to you."

The first order of business for the newly formed Jane Maas, Inc., was to have photographs taken for the advertisement selling summer tour packages at all the hotels. Leona is president of the seven Helmsley Hotels in New York: the Helmsley Palace, the Park Lane, the Harley, the St. Moritz, and the lesser-known and smaller Harley Middletowne and Harley Windsor. She also rules some twenty Harley Hotels, a national chain chiefly made up of hotels previously called Hospitality Inns. Harry and Leona renamed them by combining parts of their own names to come up with Harley. "We thought it was cute, but it was a mistake," Leona once admitted. "It's better to have a name that's known than to start from scratch."

Most of these hotels are urban properties that cater chiefly to traveling business people. Since business travel falls off sharply during the summer, it's essential for hotels to attract vacationers. And the best way to do this is with packages. We decided to show Leona in an advertisement that featured the "magic" of tour package weekends at her hotels.

Leona asked me to track down her favorite photographer. He turned out to be Norman Parkinson, named a Commander of the British Empire for his photographic achievements. Parks has photographed some of the world's most beautiful women and the English royal family for fifty years.

I reached Parks at his home near London, and set a

date for the following week in New York. We agreed to take four photographs of Leona, dressed for summer, autumn, winter, and spring, which I hoped would see us through an entire year.

"Just once," she warned me. "I'm not going through this more than once." I wonder these days, seeing the dozens of different photos of Leona that constantly appear, who at the agency is able to persuade her to pose for so many photo sessions.

Leona loaned me her car and driver so I could meet Parks at the airport. He and I had given each other a description over the telephone. "You'll recognize me," I told him. "I'm very short."

"And you'll recognize me," Parks replied. "I'm not."

We knew each other instantly. Parks is skinny as a straw and stands about six feet six.

No day with Leona was as warm and bubbly as the day of the Parkinson shoot. I arrived at the Park Lane at 7:30 A.M. to find Parks and his assistant, Chuck Zuretti, a talented young photographer in his own right, setting up lights in the rooftop garden.

Leona took me through the wardrobe choices she had already made. The summer gown, made by her favorite designer of evening wear, Julia, was perfect—gay and suitable for the carefree summer package weekends. I expressed some concern about the color of the outfit she had selected for autumn, and Leona flung open the doors of her closets for my inspection. In addition to the dozens and dozens of gowns designed by Julia ("Her dresses move with you, darling"), there were suits and dresses by Bill Blass, Valentino, Pauline Trigere, and Diane Von Furstenberg.

I remarked on the simplicity of her shoes. "The Fenton last at Saks. I buy them by the dozen and have them dyed." Leona does not believe in paying retail price for anything. One way is to buy in quantity. The other way is to bargain. Leona Helmsley deals with the great shops of the world as though they were souks in Jedda. "Learn from me, darling. If you pay the asking price for anything, you're being robbed."

At breakfast, Leona, still in her bathrobe, showed me the scar just above her breast caused when burglars stabbed her and Harry in their Palm Beach home in 1973. "At the hospital, I heard them say, 'Take care of him. She's a goner.' But I didn't want to die. I wanted to keep on living and being with my Harry." She has had a bodyguard with her ever since. (The bodyguard I knew was a former policeman. He didn't appear to be afraid of anything in the world. Except Leona.)

Leona drank juice, swallowed vitamins, munched on Special K, and told me about the daily routine that continues to keep her looking about forty years old, when best guesses put her at sixty or more. She's up at 6:30 A.M. for exercises, then swims laps in her apartment pool for one hour. Her stylist and makeup artist, Jean Louis ("I was really Juan Luis, but she hated it, so she changed my name"), does her hair and makeup, but the hairbrush or eyeliner is in Leona's hand as often as it is in his.

Leona gave me two bottles of the special moisturizer she gets from her dermatologist, and one of the buffers she uses daily to stimulate the skin. "Never pluck your eyebrows. Look at Brooke Shields. Does she pluck her eyebrows?" Plastic surgery? Never.

Over a second cup of coffee, Leona told me how she and Harry began their courtship. She had been Leona Mindy Roberts Rosenthal, born in Flatbush, attended Hunter College for a few years, became a model, married, and bore a son, Jay. (When I met Jay, he was in charge of purchasing for all the Helmsley and Harley hotels. He had already suffered several heart attacks and died, only in his early forties, in 1982.)

After her divorce, as Leona Roberts, she went into the

real-estate business and ended up working for Harry Helmsley. Don't get the idea that Leona was some kind of lowly salesperson. She was a senior vice president, making at least $500,000 a year.

Harry Helmsley approached her one evening just before the office closed. "Could you have dinner with me one night, Miss Roberts?"

Leona told him she could not. "First, because you're my boss. Second, because you're married."

Harry told her that he and his wife were divorcing, so Leona did have dinner with him. They had their first dance, and the love story began. "When Harry and I were married, he had two suits. One for winter, one for summer, both black." Leona shook her head. "Now, he's having fun." Harry Helmsley had been a Lutheran, turned Quaker, as was his first wife. Leona is Jewish.

Friends and associates who remember Harry Helmsley from his pre-Leona days agree that Leona has indeed changed his life. "He's a different man. He never used to go out, he never used to travel. Now he's enjoying life."

In addition to the Park Lane duplex and the home in Palm Springs, the Helmsleys have a jet specially decorated to Leona's taste, and own the old Billy Rose estate in Connecticut.

Leona was enjoying our breakfast conversation. She had moved from tales of their courtship and marriage to stories of how she takes care of Harry's health and diet. Everything he eats is supervised or cooked by Leona personally. Unless they are dining out, she prepares dinner for the two of them herself, in their Park Lane apartment kitchen. And she's proud of all the recipes she's created that make salt-free food taste so good. "Maybe we could do a cookbook together, darling. My recipes, your writing."

Parks arrived to tell us that the lights were ready, the props were ready, and the leading lady was needed.

Leona, helped by her maid, put on the summer dress and we began. During the long, grueling day, I watched Leona as Parks took shot after shot. She must have been exhausted, but never showed a trace of fatigue. Even for the final photo, which had Leona in a heavy winter coat trimmed with fur, she was uncomplaining about any discomfort, despite the hot lights and the warm May weather on the terrace. Inside the president of the Helmsley Hotels still lurked Mindy Roberts, model.

Two days later, we all met at the hotel to review the photographs with Parks. Leona and Harry approved them, together with the final copy and layout, and we produced our first advertisement. It showed Leona, superimposed over a photo of the courtyard of the Helmsley Palace, where a balloon man doffed his hat to her.

Leona truly does rule her hotels with an iron hand. Like the Queen in *Through the Looking-Glass,* she had only to shout "Off with his head!" and the unfortunate manager, saucier, or reservations clerk who displeased Her Majesty became an instant nonperson. During the brief months of our relationship, both the Helmsley Palace and the Harley changed managers. An article about Leona in *New York* magazine speaks of a "mass staff exodus" soon after she took over.

Life with Leona is a breathless one, and her temper can be mercurial. As we worked together closely during the summer weeks of 1981, I was present at some of her forays.

Scene: The lobby of the Helmsley Palace, where Leona accosts the young man arranging the flowers in the tall vases. The flowers, clearly, have seen better days. "Take them away and give them to a funeral parlor."

Scene: The Trianon Room of the Palace, where Leona is urging her brother, Mr. Rosenthal, manager of the residential Carlton House (another Helmsley property), to sample her newest discovery, Swedish smoked salmon. Only the day before, she had insisted that I try it, and scolded the maître d' because it was too thinly sliced. "*This* type of salmon is meant to be sliced thick."

Mr. Rosenthal, who considers himself something of a gourmet, tastes, chews, shakes his head. "It would be okay, but it's sliced too thick. Way too thick."

Leona summons the maître d', who knows from the look on her face that something is terribly wrong. It couldn't possibly be the salmon, could it? "Take this salmon away," Leona says, "and learn how to slice it the way it should be. Paper thin." The maître d' apologizes, bowing deeply.

Scene: The Central Reservations office for the seven Helmsley Hotels, just a few steps from Leona's office in the Palace. She makes a commando foray to find out why the occupancy at the Harley is not up to snuff. Leona hears one unfortunate reservations clerk inform a caller politely that there is no room at the Palace for a particular night. Leona pounces. "Why don't you say that there *is* room at the Harley. Why don't we always suggest our other hotels if they have rooms?" The reservations manager assures her this will be done from now on. "It better be," the Queen nods.

Bill Dowling told me later that Leona was absolutely right. Any well-run hotel chain automatically recommends its own. Why did the problem have to be discovered and corrected by Leona herself? She would sigh and ask you the same question.

Scene: One of the grand, high-ceilinged triplex apartments at the top of the Palace, rented by stars and sheiks. We are about to have photographs taken to send to the White House. Leona inspects the bathroom and discovers a dirty sink, a filled ashtray, a beer can. She shrieks for the housekeeper. "This room is a disgrace. I want it cleaned up, and cleaned up now!"

The housekeeper dares to argue. "It was clean when I looked at it."

"Look at it again," Leona snaps. Then, mercurial, she places a hand on the housekeeper's shoulder, her voice softens. "These suites are so important. Please help me keep them looking the way they should."

Scene: The lobby of the Palace. A tall young man in jogging attire, wearing roller skates, is *skating* across the rug heading for the guest elevators. He is tall and muscular, and given the skates, stands about seven feet high. Leona lunges at him, followed by her frantic bodyguard. "Get those skates off," she hisses at him. Then, charming: "These carpets cost a fortune. I know. I'm Leona Helmsley." The skater is impressed. Wordlessly, he kneels at her feet and removes the offending skates.

Scene: Toward the end of my tenure, I bring along two free-lance copywriters for a first meeting with Leona. We stand at the receptionist's desk on the Executive Floor, a good distance from Leona's office. Even from there we can hear her shouting at someone. The two copywriters look at me with terror. And pity.

While our honeymoon was on, Leona asked to see me almost every day that she was in New York. Sometimes I would show her creative work at her office in the Palace, often she would insist that I join her for lunch at the Palace or the Harley. And sometimes she'd ask me to stop by the fitting room of her designer, Julia, just a few steps down the hall from our office at the Graybar Building. At this point, Leona decided to redo me.

She thought I had some redeeming features, but wasn't making enough of them. She didn't like my hair. "Too short, too red." She didn't like my pantsuits. "A woman is supposed to look feminine, sweetheart. Especially when you reach a certain age. And you have a very handsome husband." She raised her eyebrows warningly. "You have to be careful."

Leona cajoled and threatened until I agreed to leave the hairdresser who had cut and colored my hair for twenty-five years, darling Mr. Lance. I pleaded loyalty. "Loyalty!" Leona snorted. "Loyalty to somebody who makes the back of your head look like that?"

She asked Phyllis Wagner to introduce me to Leslie Blanchard, the world's leading expert on hair coloring. He and I had a conference, and he agreed with Leona's analysis. My hair was too short and too red, and I must learn to use makeup. Leslie sent me off to be turned into a honey blond by Ingrid, under the . ıtchful eye of Gabriella. I was then styled by Richard and made up by Lewis. The transformation was amazing, especially as my hair grew longer.

Months later, when I became president of Muller Jordan Weiss, Phil Dougherty gave me a very generous column in *The New York Times,* complete with photograph. My sister, Susan Weston, who had not seen me for a year, called from Chicago. "Congratulations," she said. "That's a terrific article. But who's the woman in the picture?"

Now Leona turned to my wardrobe. Today, I am still grateful that she weaned me away from a daily diet of pantsuits into more feminine and softer dresses and skirts. She also gave me my first experience with a dressmaker. Julia, of course.

Her Majesty reminded me that my black velvet tuxedo had been out of place at Harry's party, so she shooed me into Julia's workroom for a few gowns suitable for evening wear. As I undressed for Julia to take my measurements, Leona scolded. "That's a terrible bra. An *ugly* bra. It looks like a *nursing* bra! A woman should look sexy, sweetheart, when she's getting dressed. Or *undressed.*" She gave me the name and style of the brassiere I was to wear henceforth. It clasps in front and is made of wispy lace.

A few weeks later Michael and I met Leona and Harry

at a black-tie gala. Leona inspected me from head to foot. Hair perfect, makeup perfect, black gown by Julia perfect. Her eyes fell to my shoes. "The shoes are all wrong. Too fussy. Why didn't you buy the Fenton last I told you to?" She sighed. "I guess I'll have to help you buy your shoes too."

Leona Helmsley gave me many things, including a crisis of confidence. She certainly did give me a more feminine persona, and I will never cease to be grateful. Neither, after he stopped chuckling at the emergence of a woman he didn't recognize, will Michael.

Although the Harley Hotel had been open for a year, it still had no brochure and the need for one was urgent. I had recently published my second book, *Better Brochures, Catalogs and Mailing Pieces,* and had supervised for five years all the hundreds of brochures for the "I Love New York" program, so a brochure for the Harley presented no challenge to me.

Leona did. We now began the Great Harley Hotel Brochure Caper. It was the beginning of the end of our relationship.

Leona gave one of her stunning regal commands about models in the brochure. "No professional models," she proclaimed. "I'm not paying those ridiculous fees for models to stand around pretending they're waiters. Use people from the hotel staff."

When Leona was out of sight, the manager of the Harley wrung his hands and wept. He was short on staff. If I took dozens of his people away to be models, he'd be out of business. I took pity on his plight, and we agreed to a compromise. We would use out-of-work actors, students, unemployed friends and relatives, and anybody else who could spare us a few hours. We gave everyone a pittance of twenty-five dollars simply to cover transportation and expenses such as baby-sitters. Leona discovered this and forbade even these nonmodel models. Jane Maas, Inc., had to pay the fees.

The photographer, Paul Elson, had been contracted to do the job by the marketing director of the Harley, Jim Bitros. I was more than pleased with the choice of Elson, since I knew he had worked with Bitros the year before on a brochure for the St. Moritz that won the award as best brochure of the year from the Hotel Sales Management Association.

Paul Elson photographed the Harley Hotel for four long days, covering everything from limousines at the circular entrance driveway to closeups ⸢f its famous fish dishes. He selected his choices from the more than eight hundred shots, mounted them on slides, placed them in slide trays, and gave them to me for presentation to Leona.

Leona looked on in silence as we showed her slide after slide: the exterior, the lobby, the bar, the grillwork leading to Mindy's Restaurant, closeups of food. Next, one of the hotel bedrooms, with a wife showing her husband the results of her shopping spree at fashionable stores located near the Harley.

Leona declared the photography unacceptable. All of it. Later she went into detail. "That bedroom was a mess," she snorted. "It looked cluttered. I like bedrooms *without* people." I have been turning that remark over in my mind for several years.

She would be happy to meet with the photographer, she told me, so she could explain to him why the shots were so bad. Then she changed her mind. "Tell him to sue me," she said. "Tell him to stand in line."

Paul Elson did indeed sue Leona. And Leona countersued me. It took about two years for the case to come to court, and I had some bad moments worrying about the possible outcome.

One day, when I was already at Muller Jordan Weiss,

the telephone rang. I answered it myself, as David Ogilvy taught all of us to do. A familiar voice was on the other end of the wire. "Would you tell me what you mean by suing me?" the Queen asked angrily.

"Gee, Leona," I said, "there's been some kind of miscommunication. I'm not suing you. *You're* suing *me.*"

The judge found Paul's photographs not only acceptable but downright excellent. Leona's attorney, listening to the verdict, looked like a victim heading for the scaffold. I knew exactly how he felt.

After the Harley brochure fiasco, my relationship with Leona began to cool. She suggested on several occasions that I didn't have a staff large enough to satisfy her needs. "Joyce Beber used to have twenty people sitting around an office brainstorming for hours." The fee paid to Jane Maas, Inc., on behalf of the Helmsley and Harley hotels was a modest one, and I couldn't afford (or house) more creative people, but I dipped into my own salary to bring in free-lance help, hoping to appease Leona.

We were inundated by requests from all the hotel managers simultaneously. The Helmsley Palace needed an advertisement for after-theater supper. The Harley wanted one for brunch. So did the St. Moritz. The Park Lane asked me to give them new signage for fire exits. I turned to Michael for help with this assignment. "That's not advertising," he said. "It's engineering."

Leona insisted on approving every word of copy. When she and Harry left for Florida or Europe, things simply went into a holding pattern. She is the only president of a major organization I have worked with in my advertising career who bothered with the body copy. But that's Leona's style. It's part and parcel of the way she runs the hotels, reading the comment cards filled out by guests, prowling the kitchens, the linen closets, the ladies' rooms. I would not be at all surprised to learn she checks the men's rooms, too.

My batting rate for copy approval by Leona began to lower. The less I saw of her, the more I would fret as meeting times approached. No more jolly lunches, no more visits to Julia. Now I would leave the Graybar Building, walk across Grand Central Station, up the escalator, through the Helmsley Walk at 230 Park Avenue, then a few short blocks to the Palace. I began to say Hail Marys quietly under my breath as I walked to these meetings, hoping Leona would not be abusive.

Dolores Zahn was incensed at what she perceived as Leona's intolerable treatment of me. "There are some people in this world," Dolores shook her finger at me "that only understand if you fight back with their weapons. Tell her where to go." For the first time in my life, however, I had the livelihood of three other people depending on how well I coped with Leona, and as much as I wanted to, I couldn't fight back.

I do believe God takes a hand. At the blackest moment of my relationship with Leona, a new account arrived at Jane Maas, Inc. Jack Rudin, head of Rudin Management, has long been a friend. At a meeting of the Building Congress, he mentioned to Michael that one of the Rudin properties, Forty One Madison, The New York Merchandise Mart, was looking for an advertising agency. I met with Carole Dixon, director of the Mart, and we began not only a client-agency relationship, but a friendship that has grown deeper every year.

Carole runs New York's (if not the world's) most prestigious building for the makers of fine china, crystal, and silver. When she became director of the Mart, Carole had experience in real estate and leasing, and, although she had no expertise in tabletop, is blessed with simple, innate good taste. She immersed herself in the tabletop industry, and pioneered events such as seminars with industry leaders, both manufacturers and buyers, which have been imitated everywhere.

With the strong support of Jack Rudin and Rudin Management, Carole has herself become a highly respected figure in the industry, and she has made Forty One Madison *the* building to be in.

I had almost forgotten what it was like to have an enthusiastic client. Fresh from the sneers of Leona ("Do you call this an ad, sweetheart?") I suddenly had the applause of Carole Dixon. The very first advertisement I wrote for Forty One Madison occurred to me while I was jogging. So many wonderful companies had showrooms there already, so many tenants had just announced they were moving there, so many department store buyers agreed that Forty One was the must building to shop at any market, that I wanted to do a "leadership" advertisement.

"What would you think," I asked Carole, "about an ad that showed the logos of your most important tenants, with the headline 'Forty One Madison. It's where the business is moving.'"

"Oh," Carole said, "oh, I love it. It's wonderful." It was like manna in the desert.

Leona Helmsley taught me how to do my hair and makeup. Carole Dixon taught me about understatement, grace under pressure, and the value of true grit. I am happy that she is still my client. I am even happier that she is, more than ever, my friend.

Another tiny account, Tumi, makers of butter-soft leather suitcases and attaché cases, also knocked on the door of Jane Maas, Inc. Tumi was run by a smart marketing man, Charlie Clifford, but even Charlie couldn't overcome customers' perception of leather luggage as heavy and expensive. We didn't prosper all that well with Tumi, although I did get a splendid attaché case for Michael. Wholesale. It was perhaps the only action of my last few months with Leona that she would have approved, had she known about it.

One of the final assignments I did out for Leona was

an advertisement for the triplex suites at the top of the Helmsley Palace. It was to be in the genre of "2 rms, Riv Vu," placed in the *Times* Real Estate section, and Leona warned me that she wanted it "tomorrow," so it could run on Sunday. The triplex rentals were hurting.

Trained in the David Ogilvy school of the persuasive powers of long copy, especially when you are selling something expensive, I was baffled by the demands of the traditional real-estate ad, where everything is abbreviated beyond recognition. But I returned to Leona the next day with a draft.

"You call this a real-estate ad?" she asked. (It was getting to be a familiar line.) "My little grandson can write a better ad than this. Now, you just go back and do this ad over again, five hundred times if you have to, but you get back here to me before this day is over with an ad I can accept."

I retraced my steps through the Hemsley Walk, Grand Central Station, into my office at the Graybar Building, and cried into my typewriter. What distinguished a great real-estate ad from a mediocre one? And, to compound the problem, Michael and I were due to join one of his clients at six that evening for a dinner before attending the Frank Sinatra benefit at Carnegie Hall. Leona knew this, as she and I had discussed the fact that she was hosting his *second* night, with a reception at the Palace.

"Tell her to take her real-estate ad and shove it into her royal ear," Dolores suggested. "She's just trying to make you miss Frank Sinatra."

I reread all the ads from the Sunday before, hoping for inspiration, and rewrote the Helmsley advertisement, making a few of the elements larger. After all, we were touting some of the most expensive real estate in New York.

It was after five when I reached Leona's office at the Palace. She and Harry had their coats on, ready to leave.

Was it possible she had forgotten this crucial ad? Leona glanced at the copy, handed it to Harry. "Amateur night," she observed.

Harry looked over the copy, then looked at me. I think he knew I had been crying. "It seems okay to me," he said. "Let's run it, and see what happens."

I got to the Frank Sinatra dinner a bit late, but I got there. The ad appeared on Sunday, and I do know it garnered telephone calls from a lot of wealthy possibilities, including one Arabian sheik and one French ambassador. I will, however, never lay claim to being a great writer of real-estate ads. I doff my hat to those who are.

The advertising done for the hotels—and for Leona— by Beber, Silverstein has made her a media celebrity. Some people snicker behind their hands, but the Helmsley Palace is sold out almost all year. *The Daily News* ranked Leona as one of New York's ten pushiest women. *The National Lampoon* ran three ads, using the same format as that of the Harley, with a Leona look-alike called "Leona M. Hellkite" for "the Harpey Hotel of New York." And young playwright Wendy Wasserstein, writing "Phil and Molly, The New Romantics" for a special issue of *The New York Times* magazine, has Phil and Molly being married in the grand ballroom of the Helmsley Palace. Presiding is "Her Royal Highness, Queen of the Helmsley." She says, "I've stood guard at their honeymoon suite. Molly will be able to see her makeup in soft light in the bathroom mirror. Phil will be put at ease by the suit hangers that detach from the closet. And if Phil and Molly decide to get remarried some day, and return to the honeymoon suite, I will keep a note of the room number."

The day that Jane Maas, Inc., closed its doors and left the Graybar Building, I discovered the music box that Leona had given as a favor on the night of Harry's birthday party, tucked away in a file drawer. It no longer played "I'm Just Wild About Harry." It had wound down.

Madame President

*T*he day before I officially became president of Muller Jordan Weiss, John Jordan, the chairman, and I met with Phil Dougherty at *The New York Times* to announce the news. Phil took lots of notes, and graciously accepted the photo I'd brought along—just in case.

The next morning, Michael says that the second we heard the sound of the *Times* hitting the floor of our elevator lobby, my feet hit the floor beside our bed. I ran out to the lobby in my nightshirt, picked up the paper, turned, and ran straight into the door. So I spent my first week as president with a black eye.

Phil's column was everything I could have wished, and more. He noted that since most women who are agency presidents founded the agencies themselves, my appointment was something of a first. He traced my career from Ogilvy & Mather through Wells, Rich, Greene, and the "I Love New York" campaign. He even mentioned Bucknell. Most important of all, he mentioned Michael!

Phil and I like each other, but I know he would not have printed that story if he didn't think it was news. He's a journalist of the old school who believes in checking sources and scooping the competition. Anyone who has felt the thrust of his Irish wit also knows how Phil delights in puncturing pomposity.

Ken Roman, who had been editor of the Dartmouth newspaper as an undergraduate, always warned me that thanking journalists for columns written in the line of duty is in poor taste. I wrote a note in that vein to Phil, concluding, "So I won't say 'thank you.' But is it okay if I tell you I think you're wonderful?"

I arrived at the agency early to confer with the construction supervisor who was cutting a doorway from my office to the office Dolores Zahn would occupy. Where did I want the door to be? Wishing Michael were there, I agonized over the decision longer than the workman thought necessary. "Okay, lady," he said, gesturing toward my office, "why don't you wait until your boss comes in and let *him* decide."

Lots of publicity followed. *Adweek,* one of our industry's important magazines, sent Maria Fisher to interview me. Fisher is a top reporter, and didn't stop until she talked to more than a dozen of my colleagues. Her article began with a charming quote from the late Marty Stern: "Every morning, I think, she jogs with husband, goes to church, makes breakfast for her family, sends the kids to school, and gets to the office at seven o'clock. At 7 A.M. she's 'up' and smiling at you." Fisher continued, "Maas is indeed 'up.' She is today the only woman in big-time advertising to head an agency she did not found."

The writer also remarked that almost every colleague of mine had noted that I have "what comes close to an obsession for organization." Good, I thought. I'm going to need it to run Muller Jordan Weiss.

When I joined the agency in September of 1982, it had been in existence for twenty-five years, and was billing just over 32 million. As I write today, just two years later, our billings are approaching 45 million. Not bad.

Andy Weiss, one of the founders, has been a friend of Michael's and mine for more than twenty years. Andy and his wife, Marilyn, rented a home near ours on Dune Road in Westhampton one summer. We met on the beach, started to talk about advertising, and never stopped. I wasn't particularly surprised when Andy called to invite me to a breakfast meeting. Every now and then, he would call and use me as sounding board for a new campaign.

We met at the Berkshire Hotel. Andy got right down to business. "What would you think about joining our agency as president?"

At that point, I was with Wyse Advertising, which had acquired little Jane Maas, Inc., chiefly through the generous efforts of its president, Lois Wyse. Lois is not only a famous copywriter ("With a name like Smucker's, it has to be good") and a chief executive officer, but also a busy wife, mother, and prolific author.

I was happy at Wyse, indebted to Lois and having fun bringing up a superb young assistant account executive, Anne Dempsey, certain to be president of an agency herself someday. However, I *did* miss being the boss.

So I told Andy Weiss his idea sounded very exciting, but before we made any decisions there would have to be lots of talks with John Jordan and Frank Muller. They would have to learn all about me, and I about them. This time around, I was going to check in with the "Network."

Nobody could have smarter or more delightful partners. Andy was a known quantity, of course. He's a creative man at heart, and probably the best example of his abilities is the "Lift a Levolor" campaign. This mnemonic device has made Levolor a household word and the dominant leader in a very low-interest category. That's why our advertising tells people to look for the name and make sure they're getting the real thing and not an imitation. Andy is also known for one of the most famous symbols in the financial world: the clasped hands for the Oppenheimer Fund.

John Jordan, our chairman, is a brilliant strategic thinker. He runs the Monsanto agricultural account, among others. We do the advertising for two of Monsanto's most important brands, Lasso and Roundup herbicides. They're extremely complex products to sell, the marketing skills needed are great, and the consumers who buy them—farmers—are sophisticated and skeptical purchasers. I feel right at home with our Monsanto clients. They remind me of the people who worked at Procter & Gamble; and, indeed, many of them are P & G alumni.

Frank Muller is a superb sailor, and he transforms many of those skills into the world of advertising. Frank knows that if you tack too often you can lose the race, so his hallmark is consistency. We have been running the same campaign for Foster Wheeler, a Fortune 500 company, for more than fifteen years. And for six years, a single advertising campaign helped to change the image of McGraw-Hill from that of a book publisher to a company in the forefront of the information business.

John, Frank, Andy, and I agreed that they would continue running their accounts, while I would run the rest of the agency. The Creative, Media, and Production departments would report to me. I'd be responsible for monitoring strategic and creative direction, and take a lead role in the pursuit of new business. Nobody guessed that my job description should have included "Chaplain."

In my first weeks at Muller Jordan Weiss, I invited the departments that were reporting to me to a series of informal lunches in our large conference room. Among the questions I asked at each lunch were, "Are you happy? Are you working too hard? Are you working hard enough? How do you feel things are going here? Is there anything we should do differently?" I was amazed and pleased by the candor of the answers, and by the general feeling that the agency was moving in the right direction.

The Accounting Department didn't report to me on paper, but my lunches were so satisfying, I invited that department to join me one day. And I asked them the same questions. "How do you feel about the way things are going here?" The Accounting Department was astounded. They told me nobody had asked them before how they felt about *anything*.

Simultaneously, I wanted to learn about every product or service that we advertised. A memo to the Account Management staff asked for brand reviews, including marketing, copy, and media strategies, for every client. One account manager, who had toiled long and hard for a demanding client, a famous name in the world of fashion, sent me a memo confessing he did not have a marketing strategy, a creative strategy, or a media strategy. "They can be summed up in one sentence," he told me. "Whatever BLANK wants, BLANK gets."

We also initiated a system so I would be copied on all conference reports and status reports. I read them *all*, and send many back to the senders with comments or questions.

My account folks know I read these reports, and they take pains to make them well-written and clear. And if I happen to run into a client, I am up-to-date on the most important issues that concern him.

Earlier in this book, I mentioned one of my favorite clients, Pete Wygant, president of Stroehmann Bakeries Inc., and now chairman of Weston Bakeries Limited, Stroehmann's parent company. He is a man I respect as a marketer and enjoy as a friend. Soon after I joined the agency, I worked with Pete on the introduction of Stroehmann's first line of "variety" breads—wheats and ryes. Although the company had long been known for its white bread, Pete knew that America was consuming less white every year. He moved fast to bring out Earth Harvest, a family of breads with no artificial preservatives, all "made from the harvest of the good earth."

We ran the advertising campaign in four test markets, using the already well-known and loved cartoon character of Grampa Stroehmann. For the first time, we added live action of a woman tasting the bread and telling Grampa how good it is. (That old Procter & Gamble "moment of affirmation" technique.) In just four weeks, we achieved 80 percent awareness of the new Earth Harvest line. No mean feat.

Pete Wygant introduced me, purely by accident, to some of the pitfalls of being a woman president. He invited the Stroehmann account group and me to the annual company sales meeting at Shawnee-on-the-Delaware.

We arrived at the hotel just as "happy hour" was beginning. All the salespeople were assembled. One scan of the room told me I was the only woman present. After cocktails, we moved into the dining room. I suggested to my agency colleagues that we separate and eat at different tables, in order to get to know as many of the salesmen as possible.

One of my dinner partners—let's call him Henry—was a route salesman from the Buffalo area. Henry had imbibed a bit too freely during cocktail hour, and now was having a few glasses of red wine with his steak.

Halfway through dinner, Henry became very friendly. "C'mon, honey, c'mon and sit on my lap."

I knew poor Henry didn't have a clue who I was, nor did any of the other salesmen at the table. I declined with a smile. Henry persisted. "You're a cute little thing. C'mon and sit on my lap."

I politely declined again, the picture of poise. "Well," said Henry, "if you won't sit on my lap, guess I'll have to sit on yours." He rose to do just that. I fled to my room.

Next morning at 8:30, we filed into the meeting room.

Henry was sitting just behind me, in the second row. He looked somewhat the worse for wear, and smiled at me sheepishly.

Pete Wygant went to the podium. He said that this meeting was momentous. It marked the first time that the advertising agency was joining them, and it indicated the deep sense in which we were marketing partners. "And now," Pete said, "to tell you about our marketing plans, I would like to introduce a famous woman in the world of advertising, the president of Muller Jordan Weiss, Jane Maas."

Henry, behind me, said, "Oh shit."

Another memorable sales meeting was held by one of our new clients, Imperial Schrade, the world's largest maker of cutlery and pocketknives. This time, three or four other women were in attendance. After two days of intensive meetings, there was a gala banquet on the last night. We learned it is a tradition at Imperial to call up to the podium every new person who has joined the company that year, and solemnly cut his necktie off. With an Imperial knife, of course.

I watched in fascination as my three agency colleagues, Andy Weiss, Ron De Luca, the management supervisor, and Patrick Fagan, Copy Group head, marched up and had their ties cut off. Then my name was called.

During what seemed an endless march to the podium, I wondered what they could do to *me*. I wasn't wearing a tie; just my gorgeous pink T. Jones silk suit. The knife flashed and I lost a lock of my hair. David Ogilvy says he is the only head of an agency who actually bled for a client (he donated his blood to test the cleaning powers of a detergent). However, I am surely the first who has been scalped for one.

My most important commitment as president of Muller Jordan Weiss is to our clients, to see that our creative product, marketing, media, and research are all first

class. My second commitment is the pursuit of new business. As my co-author Ken Roman puts it, "In advertising, new business isn't a matter of life or death. It's more
important than that."

The first piece of new business we acquired after I
joined the agency was Stimorol, an imported Danish
chewing gum. Mike Stone, then head of the company,
wanted creative work that would make the gum unique.
We presented to him several times in November. On
Thanksgiving Day I had the temerity to call him at home
and tell him how much we wanted his account.

Mike called me the following Monday. "Anybody who
takes the time on Thanksgiving Day to make the kind of
call you did, deserves the business. You're our agency."
Leftover turkey never tasted so good.

Stimorol, which had been positioned as "the chewing
gum for the rich," didn't have a large advertising budget,
but the idea of an upscale chewing gum tickled the fancy
of feature writers everywhere, and Mike got millions of
dollars of free publicity. I. Magnin in San Francisco devoted a window display to Stimorol. *The New Yorker* magazine wrote about it. Addicted Stimorol chewers all over
the country who couldn't find the gum at their local
candy stores wrote in to order cases of it.

We came up with some new ideas for print and radio.
"The only gum insured against loss, theft, or acts of
God." Stimorol chewers had only to write in explaining
why their gum was lost, stolen or strayed, and it would be
replaced. Letters poured in. A San Francisco user declared that an earthquake made the ground open up in
front of her, enveloped her Stimorol, and closed again. A
man in New York gave us a vivid description of a gorilla
that resembled King Kong grabbing his Stimorol. Stimorol sales began to take off. And I encourage gum chewing at the office, as long as it's Stimorol.

It was quickly apparent to me that one of the biggest

challenges of the new job was time management. My own time. I turned to Ken Roman, a superb manager. Ken advised, "You've gotten where you are by saying 'Yes. Yes, I can. Yes, I can write a white paper on the future of the coffee business. Yes, I can have it for you in two weeks. Yes, if you need it faster I can work all weekend and deliver it on Monday.'" Ken concluded, "Now stop saying 'Yes' and start saying 'No.'" It is the most difficult advice I've ever tried to follow.

I do say "No" now to job seekers not related to me either by blood or marriage, client contact, Bucknell, or Fordham. I say "No" to small speeches unless they are requests from friends. I say "No" (alas) to almost all restaurant lunches unless they are "musts." Lunch hour, like the time before nine and after five, is golden time to get work done without telephones ringing. When I do lunch with friends, we usually have a hard-boiled egg in my sunny office.

Breakfast meetings are better than lunches. The restaurants are quieter, people don't drink, and more is accomplished in a shorter time. I believe dinner should be a purely social occasion.

In the Wells, Rich, Greene days, I always came into the office about eight, typed away at my old manual, then handed stuff to Dolores when she arrived at nine. As my in-box at Muller Jordan Weiss began to tower over me, I started coming in at 7:30. Dolores, in self-defense, began appearing at 8:30. We were still falling behind. One morning Dolores came in to find I had arrived at 6:30 and had twenty-nine different letters and memos for her to type.

"Listen," she said, shaking that warning Irish finger under my nose. "If you keep coming in earlier and earlier, and I keep coming in earlier and earlier, we'll both be here in the middle of the night. Something is going to have to give, and I'll be quick to tell you it isn't going to be me." I declared that 7:30 would be my earliest arrival point—most of the time.

One terrific timesaver is a ploy taught me by David Ogilvy. He urged his heads of offices not to summon people to them. "This frightens them," he said. "You go to *their* offices." This practice also allowed David to beat a speedy retreat any time he wanted to. When people are in your office, you can be trapped.

A nifty trick that is especially effective for women is to stand up and remain standing when an unexpected visitor enters. It's hard for a man to sit down and settle in for a long chat when *I* am standing up. Dolores guards my door like a dragon, so few people manage to sneak by. When they do, though, up I pop.

It pays to work in trains, planes, and cars. I wrote much of this book on long car and train rides to and from Williamsport, Pennsylvania, and Hartford, Connecticut.

Writing the word "Hartford" reminds me to report that we were indeed awarded the account by the Society for Savings Bank of Hartford. Mary Chase, vice president, called the week after the presentation. "Do you have your running shoes on?" she asked. "You're going to be our agency."

We all hugged one another, ordered up champagne, and went to work. Focus group interviews with many of the bank's customers and potential customers told us that the theme "Society is on the move" was well received and suggested that the bank was innovative. The running shoe as symbol added an extra dimension. Some people even said that the idea of bankers wearing running shoes made them seem more warm and human. Todd Ikard, executive vice president, and the warmest and most human of bankers, always smiled when people in the research groups voted for the running-shoe campaign. It was his favorite from the day we presented it, and I suspect he had a hunch that it would generate the kind of excitement Society needed.

Now, could we convince the bankers at Society that they should actually wear blue Nikes for a whole month when the campaign launched? We held more focus group sessions with the bank staff, and found many were for the idea, but some against it. Elliott Miller, president of Society, carried the day. He declared that he didn't care what anybody else did. *He* was going to wear running shoes. That settled that. Gwen Gionfriddo, advertising manager, had the awful job of getting shoe sizes from every single person on the staff.

We filmed the commercial, which was the brainchild (as was the entire campaign) of creative director Jerry Colman. It was enhanced on location by head of production Aaron Ehrlich, who improves every storyboard he touches.

Mary Chase, Peter Mulligan, director of marketing, and Frank Litwin, director of market management, invited me up to Hartford for lunch two weeks after the campaign began. "Wear your running shoes," they said.

We walked a few blocks from their offices to a restaurant. At least a dozen people commented on our shoes. "There goes Society." "Hi there, Society." "We see you're on the move." I told my clients I hadn't seen word of mouth like that since the days of "I Love New York."

The running-shoe campaign was a success on all counts. Research showed that awareness of the bank almost quadrupled in just four weeks, and the attitudes of current and potential customers reflected Society's change from a conservative savings bank to a bank "on the move."

Mel Kalfus, management supervisor on the Society account, is also director of marketing services for Muller Jordan Weiss, and the man who made the agency computer literate. That includes me! I am writing this book on a portable IBM-PC, using WordPerfect software. Nobody but Mel would have had the patience to wean me from my battered old manual.

Mel received a call early in 1984 asking us to be one of several agencies making speculative creative presentations to the Italian Shoe Center, a division of the Italian Trade Commission.

We worked on marketing plans and campaigns for two weeks. The great day dawned, and our Italian clients arrived, together with two English-speaking members of the marketing group who served as interpreters. Mel, a soft-spoken intellectual, had perceived that some knowledge of Italian might be helpful, and immersed himself at Berlitz. He was able, in Italian, to extend a gracious welcome to our guests and read a marketing plan.

I was next at bat, and presented copies of *How to Advertise* in its newly published Italian edition, *Come Fare Pubblicita*. Then I showed the television storyboards and layouts for print advertisements. It was rough going for everyone. I would read a sentence. The translator would render it into Italian. Then I'd read another sentence.

I melted inside my suit. Commercials that we thought were screamingly funny didn't get a smile. Commercials we thought were serious got laughs. One storyboard received no reaction at all. Normally I enjoy being on my feet presenting. That day I was glad to sit down.

I looked with pity at account supervisor Susan Bodiker, who was going to present the media plan. She would have the ordeal of talking about gross rating points and impressions, waiting for the translation, then having any questions translated back into English.

Susan asked one of the interpeters if it would be appropriate for her to present the media plan in French. She was told that the Italians all understood French perfectly. So Susan, without preparation, launched into a flawless and fluent presentation of the most technical kind. She paused only once. *"Comment est-ce qu'on dit* 'test market' *en français?"* she asked.

"Test market," the interpreter replied.

After a light lunch in our conference room, catered by Mangia (cold pasta salad with basil, assorted Italian cheeses, fruit, and Soave), we escorted our potential clients to the elevator.

One of the most senior members of the delegation, Dr. Soana, patted me on the shoulder. *"Benissimo,"* he said. I understood that word.

"Mel," I said, after they'd left, "I think we've got a shot at it. They told me *benissimo."*

"Alevai," Mel responded. That's an almost untranslatable Yiddish word that means, roughly, "It should only happen."

It happened. Two weeks later we were officially named the agency for the Italian Shoe Center. The entire Creative Department lined up outside my office to volunteer for the account. They seem to have a sixth sense about clients who are going to welcome innovative creative work. Gianluigi Liberati, director of the Center, and Colette Hughes, associate director, are clients like that.

They approved a rather daring commercial in which a snorkel lens camera explores its way through hundreds of green, white, and red shoes, then pulls back to reveal the shoes forming the Italian flag, with the words "Made in Italy" beneath it. Copywriter Chuck Borghese and art director Scott Sager kept the words to a minimum. "The finest, most fashionable shoes you can buy don't have to be expensive. They just have to say 'Made in Italy.'"

The commercial went on air in two test markets, in cooperation with local department stores. It worked. As one store manager reported to me with a straight face, "The shoes walked right out the door." We prepared to "roll out" to more markets.

The most embarrassing new business presentation I've

made at this agency so far was to Schrade, famous makers of pocketknives. We were already handling the advertising for Imperial cutlery, and doing a good job, so I was pleased when Marty Zorn, president of Imperial Schrade, and Jim Economos, advertising manager, asked us to make a presentation for the pocketknife business.

We had a number of different approaches. One, a particular favorite of mine, showed a woman holding the pocketknife, with the headline "You can tell a man by his Schrade." *I* thought the line suggested that a man wasn't a real man unless he carried a Schrade knife. Later I learned it suggested a lot more.

I stood in the client's conference room and presented the campaign. Mark Gardiner, sales director for Schrade, kept trying to conceal a grin. The more ads I presented, the more he grinned. Now I was reading the body copy, which was written from a woman's point of view about how she imagined her husband's activities on a fishing trip. It went ". . . and sometimes in his tent, he'll whip out his Old Timer and . . ." I got no further. My audience exploded with howls of glee. All of them, "Uncle Henry" Baer, Marty Zorn, Wally Gardiner, Jim Economos, all just whooping and shouting with tears in their eyes. Suddenly, the meaning of the *double entendre* became clear to me. I cast a horrified look at my agency colleagues, Andy Weiss, Pat Fagan, and Ron DeLuca, who smiled innocently back. They had known all along.

We were awarded the Schrade account, but we didn't produce the woman-testimonial approach.

One crisp day in January, our old friend attorney Steve Kumble asked me to be chairman of the annual dinner for the Governor's Committee on Scholastic Achievement. This group was founded by Robert Wagner when he was mayor of New York, and devoted its efforts to raising scholarship funds for New York college students.

I accepted, and inwardly vowed this would be the best-attended dinner ever, or I would die in the attempt.

The honoree was John Tishman, of real-estate fame, whose organization was located right in our building, 666 Fifth Avenue. (It may be more appropriate to say that we are located in John Tishman's building.)

I worked on the event every day for three months, checking in daily with executive director Blanche Gottlieb on the latest head count, cajoling friends and clients to take tables. Alan Gelb, a partner at Finley, Kumble, Wagner, and a vice chair of the dinner, convinced me that the entertainment would be more fun if it were a tribute to John Tishman, with lyrics specially written about him. Thanks, "Uncle Alan." It was like mounting a Broadway show.

Larry Forde, Broadway director and stage manager, "volunteered" to stage the entertainment. Lyricist Michael Rose, with some help from Tishman staffers, wrote half-a-dozen new lyrics to old tunes. The cast included Kitty Carlisle Hart, who was preparing for a Broadway run in *On Your Toes* and sounded fabulous; Hugh Carey singing "New York, New York"; members of the Building Congress; and singing plumber Marty Haber, who brought the house down with his own version of *Fiddler on the Roof's* "If I Were a Rich Man." "If I Were a Tishman."

The morning of the dinner I knew we were a success. We'd sold 120 tables. A record. That night, Steve Kumble called me up to the podium and introduced me in glowing terms. All I could think about was how exhausted I was and how my feet hurt. I thanked everybody who had made the dinner such a success: the Tishman organization, the entertainers, Steve Kumble.

"And most of all," I concluded, "I would like to thank one man for all his patience and understanding during the last three months. My husband, Michael Moose."

There was a long silence. "Michael," I whispered into the microphone, "give me another twenty-five years and I promise I'll learn how to pronounce it."

My partners sometimes ask me why I spend so much time and energy on *pro bono* activities. Well, first of all, I enjoy it. It's another window on the world. What fun to sit with Dennis O'Brien, president of Bucknell (now president of the University of Rochester), and discuss Plato. What fun to sit with Father O'Hare, president of Fordham, and discuss, not Plato, but basketball. Gary Sojka, now president of Bucknell, waxes poetic about microbiology. I tell my partners that good deeds bring their own rewards. "Bread cast upon the waters . . ."

Sanford Zimmerman, who owns Cohoes Specialty Store near Albany, was looking for an advertising agency early in 1984. He remembered me, because I had served with his wife, Eve, on the board of the Girl Scout Council of Greater New York. We had breakfast at the University Club, and Sandy asked me if we'd like to be his agency. Would we ever! The entire creative department lined up again to volunteer, and I knew we had an exciting account on our hands.

Sandy Zimmerman generates excitement. He was chairman of Abraham & Straus for some years, then bought Cohoes in 1979. It was already an institution, to which people came in busloads for good clothes at 20 percent off regular price. Sandy dressed the store up, added lots of designer labels, installed pretty, private dressing rooms, and trained salespeople to take care of customers the way they used to in the good old days.

Sandy had opened a "Cohoes Commons" in Hartford in 1983. Now he was planning two more, in Providence and Rochester. (And, knowing Sandy, I guessed this was just the beginning.) We needed advertising that conveyed not only the off-price message, but the range of designer fashions available.

Pat Fagan, art director Carol Flynn, and producer Aaron Erlich came up with the winning idea. Don't show the store, they appealed. Instead, have a Cohoes couple dressing up for a night on the town. The shopping bags, the shoe boxes, the tags—all say Cohoes. We never even see the couple, just parts of them: an ear, an ankle, the nape of a neck. Elegant, first-class advertising, just like the product it was selling. Phil Dougherty came by for a preview and wrote a wonderful column headlined "MJW's chic new campaign for Cohoes."

Frank Lloyd Wright once said, "Behind every great building is a great client." That's true of advertising, too. You cannot produce great work without a client who demands it. No client is more demanding, or more exhilarating, than Sandy Zimmerman. And his alter ego, a woman of quintessential good taste, my Girl Scout buddy Eve.

Other potential clients were becoming more and more aware of Muller Jordan Weiss, and its creative energy. David Seiniger asked us to do the advertising for his Marisa Christina fashions. George Dempster, former Commissioner of Commerce for New York State, tapped our agency for his New York Helicopter advertising. We wanted more people to know that on most airlines, if you fly first or business class, you fly New York Helicopter *free*. And even if you fly economy class, the helicopter flight usually won't cost you more than a taxi fare. I will *never* sit sweating in traffic again, wondering whether I'll make the flight on time. Try it. You'll like it.

Clients often ask me what it takes to be a good client. I tell them it's hard; good clients are rare. Some of our clients I haven't yet mentioned embody the traits that agencies admire. There's Dave Robinson of Stroehmann, who always asks for that extra mile, and always says thank you for the effort. Kenn Donnellon of Blair, who plans ahead and never makes his agency work all night to meet a deadline. Kenn also is human enough to show enthusiasm when he likes something. I love Paul Berko of Walden Farms for always being gentle with creative people, and Marty Zorn of Imperial Schrade for telling it like it is.

Ken Roman and I say in our book that creative people do their best work on accounts they like, for clients they like to work with. *Good clients.* Not necessarily *easy* clients. At Muller Jordan Weiss we're lucky to have so many clients we like.

The agency grew, with growth of current clients and the addition of new business. We began to be known as a hot creative agency and my phone started to ring with queries from potential advertisers. One came from a shy gentleman who ran a winery in upstate New York. He didn't have a *huge* budget for advertising, he admitted, but it had doubled over the year before, and he thought we might be interested. A New York state wine. My ears perked up.

"How much do you plan to spend in the next twelve months?" I asked.

"I'm going to blow the works," he told me. "Five hundred."

"Five hundred thousand dollars" I repeated after him, getting ready to tell him we might be a bit too large for him.

"Five *hundred*," he said. "Mostly barn signs."

There were other calls from big potential clients, calls that made Dolores invoke Mel's *alevai.* "From your mouth to God's ear—alevai—" she'd whisper, and cross herself. I figured we had everything possible going for us.

One of our most important assets was the addition of talented young people in all areas of the agency. I wish I could mention them all, but let four serve as examples. Art director Dale Calvert, who won a coveted award for us with his work for Blair. Mailroom manager Steve

Price, who knows an agency is often judged by the efficiency of its mailroom. Marty Trachtenberg, head of traffic, who works from dawn to dusk with good cheer and good sense. (Marty is not related to my buddy Steve Trachtenberg, president of the University of Hartford, but they share the same energy.)

And there's account supervisor Chris Moseley, who made the same transition that I once did, from television to advertising, and found her element. Chris runs *five* demanding accounts and is always the first to volunteer for more. When David Ogilvy advised us all to hire people who want our jobs because they make us look good, he must have had Chris in mind.

Dolores left reluctantly for Florida and retirement (Norman Zahn's, not hers. Dolores will *never* retire) in the fall of 1984, but before she did, she found a fabulous replacement. Judith Halleran, known as Jude.

My old friend and client, Tucker Halleran, with whom I'd worked at General Foods on the Good Seasons account back in the Ogilvy days, suddenly popped back into my life. Tuck had taken a year off from his management consulting practice in Florida to write a book. Well, actually, most first-time authors would have settled for one book, but Tuck wrote two. Mysteries. Damn good ones, too, both with the same hero, one Cam MacCardle. The first is *A Cool, Clear Death,* the second *Sudden Death Finish.*

Tucker made a date to have coffee with me one morning. It was the only day I truly had to take off as a sick day since Jenny Maas was born. Dolores went out to tell Tucker that, unhappily, there was a last-minute hitch, and coffee would have to be postponed. Irish eyes met Irish eyes. An hour later, Dolores and Tucker were huddled over coffee, while Tuck explained that he and his wife were moving from Florida back to New York, and she was a super executive assistant. She is.

Dolores taught Jude how to wave her finger under my

nose and scold me if I come in earlier than 7:30. Jude, who was Tucker's proofreader, brings the same raised eyebrow over bad grammar that Dolores did, and has added some touches of her own. Since she thinks I am undernourished, we now have a fully stocked refrigerator in her office. I expect a microwave oven any day.

All work and no play makes for droopy advertising agencies and disgruntled troops. Every now and then we have an office party to celebrate lots of events, and toast birthday children, new parents or newlyweds, promotions, award winners.

One summer, feeling that it would add to agency "togetherness," we entered the Manufacturer's Hanover Corporate Challenge Race in Central Park. The course is 5 kilometers, or 3.5 miles, and the entry form announced that there would be a prize for the fastest men's team, fastest women's team, and fastest president. Our team cocaptains, account executives John Betancourt and Greg Gomes, called to ask the race committee if there were separate awards for male and female presidents.

They were told no, as apparently there had been no women presidents running in previous years. "There is one running this year," John and Greg told them. So the race committee agreed to have an additional prize for the most fleet-footed woman president.

I thought the race involved only advertising agencies. Unless Mary Wells Lawrence suddenly put on her running shoes, I figured, all I need to do was crawl over the finish line.

Our team of seven men and three women practiced running the course for weeks before, with great training help from Greg Gomes, who brought the same care and energy to that job as he does to his work on Society for Savings.

The evening of the race, I had a car and driver pick up the women runners, the cheerleaders (Dolores Zahn and

Lu Centers), and a case of beer. We arrived at the park, and I realized that it wasn't just an advertising race. Everybody was there, from giants like AT&T to the smallest boutique.

Although Michael and I jog, this was my first race. The gun sounded and off I went, feeling pleased that I was able to pass many women, a number of them cute young things at that. From Tavern on the Green up to 90th Street and Fifth, back down to 72nd Street and the final half-mile stretch.

I saw the finish line, saw the big helium-filled red and white balloons that marked the Muller Jordan Weiss brigade, heard my buddies cheering, "Go, Jane, go!" Through my head flashed visions of Phil Dougherty's column with the headline: MAAS FASTEST PRESIDENT.

I finished the 3.5 miles in 35 minutes and 37 seconds, but I lost to a young woman who, they told me, was about two minutes faster. "Whoever you are," I thought to myself, "watch out. Because Jane Maas is coming at you." Next year I plan to win, whatever it takes.

That's the way I feel about advertising. Muller Jordan Weiss is growing to be the best agency in New York, with the finest client list and the brightest, most spirited people. And, if we keep going the way we are, maybe one day the name will be Muller Jordan Weiss & Maas. Or even, and doesn't it sound pretty, Maas Muller Jordan Weiss.

Alevai.

Working and Loving it . . .
and Loving

*S*hortly after I became president of Muller Jordan Weiss, I was interviewed by one of the many advertising industry publications. The reporter wanted to find out my priorities in terms of career, husband, and children. (Why don't reporters ever ask *men* questions like that?)

I replied that during all the years I was scrambling up the career ladder, my priorities had been clear. Career first, husband second, children third. "Now," I added serenely, "now that I've made it to the place I want to be, my priorities are reversed. Husband first, children second, career third."

Humbug.

Just two months after that interview, Michael and I went off to a tropical paradise for a brief but long-planned vacation. A phone call came from the office. Could I cut the vacation short by three days (three days out of five!) to return to New York for a new business presentation? Of course I could.

"I'm so sorry, darling," I said to Michael, but we're going to have to go back three days early."

"I'm so sorry, darling," Michael replied, "but *you're* going to have to go back three days early."

We made the new business presentation, but we didn't

get the business. Michael stayed on, played a few rounds of golf with the CEO of a big corporation, and got a major architectural project. There's a moral in there somewhere.

David Ogilvy reminds us that most psychiatrists believe that everyone should have a hobby. He urges his people to make their hobby *advertising*. I also agree with him that if you stay home, tend your roses, and care for your family, you may be a better person for it, but you will probably not rise to the top of your profession.

Put your career first.

This is particularly difficult advice for women who are married, and even more difficult for those with young children. However, even in these days of raised consciousness, there are few successful men who call in to tell the boss, "Sorry I can't make the client meeting, but my kid is in his class play." It's still easier for a woman to make this excuse, but I don't think we should.

I mentioned earlier that when Kate was born I took off two whole weeks. When I left New York Hospital after Jenny arrived, four years later, I met our housekeeper in the lobby, handed over the baby, and headed straight to the office. In those days, mothers with children under six or eight simply did not work, except out of dire economic necessity. So I was out to prove a point.

Now I suggest to my young women friends who are pregnant that they consider spending three to six months at home. No longer, though, or you risk falling behind, getting rusty, and leaving the mainstream.

This advice doesn't mean a successful working mother has to be the Wicked Witch of the West. I have spent lots of hours watching Kate or Jenny as the third tree from the left in a school play, in a fashion show for the annual fair, or singing in the glee club at a morning assembly.

Living in New York City within a ten-minute taxi ride of their school was an advantage. (Michael and I agreed early on that as long as I wanted to work, we would live in the city.) I always arrived breathless at Nightingale-Bamford, and grabbed a seat in the balcony of the auditorium. Kate or Jen, whoever was performing, would scan the audience. My reward was always the broadest beam of pleasure bestowed on any mother. Worth double the taxi fare!

When Kate was in first grade, only two out of the twenty-eight mothers in the class worked full time. The school encouraged us moms to hang out at the local coffee shop for the first few days, so we'd be nearby in case one of our daughters were homesick. The other working mother and I snuck off, boarded the Fifth Avenue bus, and wondered if we were causing irreparable damage.

I don't believe my career has hurt Kate or Jenny one whit. In fact, they both pay me the nice compliment of seeing me as a role model. Kate wants to be an advertising copywriter. Jenny wants to be president of an agency. I suspect they will both make it.

There are two essential ingredients for combining a successful career with a successful marriage and family. The first is a sympathetic husband. The second is a housekeeper (preferably one who lives in), who is loving enough to be a surrogate mother and energetic enough to take care of everything else. And I mean *everything*.

Michael has always been extraordinary in his pride in my career and his willingness to lend a hand. And those were the days when men didn't know how to change a diaper and were proud of it. On these inevitable Monday mornings when our housekeeper would call in sick, Michael and I had a plan. If I had an important meeting and he didn't, then he would stay home until a baby-sitter arrived. If, on the other hand, *he* had an important meeting, I would stay home. If we both had important meetings, there was no question about who waited for the sitter and missed the meeting. Me. It was then, and still is today, easier for a woman to call and explain that she'll be late because of a baby-sitter than it is for a man.

The other ingredient for managing home and career is a live-in housekeeper. I stress the word *live-in,* knowing that it means the added expense of an extra bedroom. Many couples also fear a loss of privacy, which we have never suffered. A sleep-out housekeeper doesn't work nearly as well. There are too many mornings when you'll need to be at your office at the crack of dawn; too many evenings when you'll suddenly need to work late; too many last-minute trips.

Don't think this talk of housekeepers is meant to sound like "Advice to the Rich." It's part of the dues a woman pays for success. During my early years as working mother, most of my take-home salary went to our housekeeper. And for at least a few years after Kate was born, Michael and I gave up other pleasures to afford that extra bedroom.

Our housekeeper, Carmen Dyce (known as Mabe), has been with us for twenty-one years now. From the beginning, we worked on a five-day-week arrangement. Every Friday night, Mabe went home to Brooklyn, and Michael and I took over. When the children were young, I had to be up every morning of the year by at least 7 A.M. Sleeping until I woke up seemed to me the most blissful state imaginable.

Once a year, Michael and I would ask Mabe to work over the weekend, pack our bags, and sneak off to the old Savoy Plaza Hotel. Our friends thought these weekends were really sexy. All we did, in fact, was sleep.

Few people I know grew up with household help. So most working mothers, including me, learned "on the job" about successful relationships with housekeepers. Friends always gasp when I say Mabe has been with us for more than twenty years. They think it's a miracle.

The truth is mutual respect and some guidelines worked out by trial and error.

For instance, don't assume that your housekeeper keeps house the way you do. Mabe came to us straight from Jamaica, and we had differences in lifestyle. The multinozzled vacuum cleaner was a mystery to Mabe at first. Even now, she still prefers the Jamaican cleaning method. Start at the farthest reach of the apartment with a good, stiff broom and sweep debris before you until finished. By the time Mabe reaches the kitchen, the mound is usually larger than she is.

I can't stand watching Mabe clean house her way, but that fact led us to the most important guideline of all. I respect her domain, ask her when I want something special done, and then leave her alone to get on with it. A ship can't have two captains, so I run the office and Mabe runs the apartment.

American cooking was a hurdle for Mabe at first. Jamaican cooks (and Mabe is a fine one) tend to marinate all meat overnight, then cook it for hours until it's well done. This may be a swell technique for preparing goat, but Michael was horrified the first time Mabe served up a filet mignon.

Mabe can now broil a steak *bleu*, but she's never learned to like it. For years, we thought Mabe preferred not to join us for meals because she was shy. She was too polite to tell us she couldn't stand meat as blood rare as we liked it. She reminded me of the Texan contestant on "Name That Tune" who complained about the way New Yorkers liked their steaks. "I seen a cow hurt wors'n that get up and walk away," he said.

Michael says his favorite memories of Mabe will always be of Thursday mornings—declared wash days. Mabe enters the bedroom, strips the bed, strips the closet, strips the towels, all at high speed. Michael is waiting for the day when she will automatically strip him too.

Different families have different needs, and should search for housekeepers who can fill them. My top priority was finding someone who would be a loving second mother. So Mabe and I agreed that if one of the girls were sick and she had to spend most of her day tending to the patient, I wouldn't snivel if I came home to an untidy house. I wish I could say I have *always* lived up to that bargain.

The Maas award for most difficult hor 2keeping position to fill goes to Peggy Vandervoort Kumble, one of the very few women in the world who buys, sells, and breeds thoroughbred race horses professionally. Her husband, attorney Steve Kumble, is the managing partner of Finley, Kumble, Wagner, Heine, Underberg, Manley & Casey, America's second-largest law firm. (Also its longest-named law firm?) Steve loves to entertain at home, and has a mania for spotless crystal. Peggy swears that when Steve has a bout of insomnia, she can hear him clanking around their bar in the middle of the night, holding Baccarat goblets up to the light, inspecting for spots. So Peggy specifies help who can cook brilliantly and have a passion for gleaming glassware.

Michael, Mabe, and I discussed our policy on sick days and vacations. Some employers I know don't believe in paying household help for days taken because of illness. These same Scrooges then wonder why they can't keep good help! As to vacation policy, I told Mabe we would do approximately what my own employer, Ogilvy & Mather, was then doing. Two weeks off after the first year, three weeks after five years, four weeks after ten years. We never discussed what amount of vacation would be due her after twenty years, and Mabe hasn't brought it up. I suspect we'll have that conversation after she reads this book.

How long will you need a housekeeper? My answer is: as long as you have children living at home. Even an eighteen-year-old should not have to be home alone with a fever. And there's something else to consider. By the time your children are grown up and off to college, you will probably be so accustomed to the joy of being cared for that you are hooked for life.

No number of guidelines can take the place of years of caring and affection. Bless you, Mabe, for all the times I've wept on your shoulder, all the times you forgave me for venting on you a crossness concealed at the office all day, all the times you made last-minute forays in rain or snow for that matching thread to sew a tear in an evening gown. Bless you for hanging in all these years. I promise never to tease you again about being the only person in the world who wears a wool cap indoors in the summer.

Now, how do you mix a good career with a good marriage? After twenty-seven years of marriage, having worked during every one of them, I feel I'm a pretty fair authority on the subject.

We air important differences, and ignore small ones. Soon after we were married, Michael suggested that I learn to golf so we could enjoy playing together. Since I went around in the low 150s, in the woods all the way, it was more like jungle warfare than a sport. By the eighteenth hole, I was usually in tears.

It took a psychiatrist to make me give up the game.

"Simply tell Michael you don't want to play golf anymore," advised Dr. Mort Kurland.

"I can't do that," I wailed. "He thinks I love it."

"Blame me," Dr. Kurland countered. "Say I think it's too hard on your nerves."

I screwed my courage to the sticking-place. "Michael," I quavered, "I have something awfully important to tell you. I'm going to give up golf."

"That's terrific," Michael said, obviously relieved. "I'm surprised you kept at it so long when you're so terrible."

We *did* want to find some activity we enjoyed doing together, and tried sailing. Michael fell in love with a trim racing boat, the Flying Scot, so we bought one, christened it *The Mops* (my nickname, a short form of Flopsy Mopsy Cottontail, given me when I used to read *Peter Rabbit* to the girls), and joined the Westhampton Yacht Squadron. The first time we raced also marked the first time we ever sailed. I was reading Michael instructions from a book on racing about how to get the spinnaker sa.. up. Before I reached the end of the first paragraph, the spinnaker was up, and so was Michael, his feet yanked right off the deck by the force of the wind.

Our "crew" that day was Jeannie Jenkins, destined to become a best friend. Jeannie, an experienced sailor who must have been thunderstruck by our blunders, was her tactful self. "Great going, Michael," she complimented him, as he hung there in the breeze. "I've never seen a spinnaker set that way before, but you're looking good."

Thereafter, it became my job to put up the dreaded spinnaker pole. It was scary, out there on deck, standing on tiptoes to attach the wretched thing while the boat pitched. Michael and I had the only awful fights of our marriage while racing *The Mops*.

"Dammit," he'd shout at me. "You're supposed to be a Phi Beta Kappa. How come you can't get up the damned spinnaker pole?"

We decided to sell the boat.

Then we took up jogging. It is just the sport we had been looking for. We run five miles almost every day. (We don't run in heavy rain or if the wind-chill factor is less than ten below.) Weekdays we run around the Central Park resevoir; weekends we circle the entire park.

Running on vacations is a marvelous way of seeing more of any city we visit. In Paris, we have run from the

Ile St. Louis as far as the Bois de Boulogne. Another time, we were jogging toward Vincennes, got lost in the maze of railroad yards around the Gare de Lyon, and were rescued by an English-speaking Indian from Madras. In Rome, we set our all-time distance record: from our hotel to the basilica of St. Paul Outside-the-Walls, about twelve miles.

Jogging led us to another activity we enjoy: simply walking. Weekends, we walk all around New York. From our apartment on 92nd and Park Avenue down to Little Italy for lunch at Luna. Down to the Brooklyn Bridge and across to Brooklyn Heights, then lunch at Gage & Tollner. Down Columbus Avenue to Greenwich Village and Soho, and the Soho Charcuterie. We always reward ourselves with long lunches after long walks, free from guilt about calories.

Michael has taught me to raise my sights and look up as we walk. Second stories and above of older buildings are covered with wondrous gargoyles and caryatids, murals and sculpture. I pity anyone who doesn't have a built-in architect as guide.

We've also agreed that it's no disgrace for one of us to enjoy an activity the other doesn't. Michael continues to play golf. I do not begrudge him his weekend matches in Westhampton, or even his two-day outings to that male chauvinist bastion Pine Valley, where good golfers are said to go when they die.

When Michael is out of town, I go to the theater with a woman friend. My favorite theater-going buddies are Carole Dixon, friend and client; Jeannie Jenkins, my Westhampton friend, who dashes in on the jitney; and Judy Jordan Oppenheimer, gifted English teacher and favorite friend, with whom I see many plays, especially when they're Shakespeare. My youngest friend is Bess O'Brien, herself a gifted actress, who is such satisfying company. Even a mediocre play, imperfectly performed, will move Bess to applause. A superb play with a great cast makes her almost hysterical with awe and joy. When we saw Christopher Plummer as Iago, I thought Bess would levitate from her chair.

Michael and I are ruthless about turning down invitations. We find that more than two evenings out in any given week is hard on our waistlines and our dispositions. (Of course there are weeks when it's impossible to avoid a string of events; when they occur, we get home as early as possible and remind ourselves we'll be tired.)

We do our entertaining during the we、., and almost never go out on Saturday nights. Nor do we leave home on New Year's Eve. When friends invite us to toast in the new year with them, we decline politely and send a telegram: HAPPY NEW YEAR FROM THE BED OF JANE AND MICHAEL MAAS.

We take lots of mini-vacations. We find we simply can't get away for longer than a week, so we usually aim for October in Italy, France, or England. October is oyster time in Paris, truffle time in Venice, and game season everywhere. One October, while staying at the Villa Cipriani in Asolo, north of Venice, we drove to Bassano del Grappa to visit a restaurant famous for its game. There, for the first—and last—time of my life, I ate uccelli (known in France as ortolans), tiny birds the size of hummingbirds. Proper etiquette calls for picking them up by the beak and eating them head and all. Crunch!

Long weekends, Thursday through Monday, are perfectly possible for destinations no further than London or Paris, especially when bargain fares are available. We have also discovered how good four or five days at a health spa can make us feel. Or a quick trip to a Caribbean island—*any* Caribbean island in January or February, when you think winter will never end.

Most important of all, we have a home in Westhampton that is utterly carefree. It's a mile inland, surrounded by pine trees and wild blueberry bushes. We fall asleep to the distant sound of the sea, and wake up to crows and jays and bobwhite quail. Three days out there, any season of the year, is enough to rejuvenate us. We pull the house around us like a big comforter, and don't crawl out until it's time to go back to the city.

We plan our weekends the way we do our vacations, with as much glee in the deciding as in the doing. We think ahead about meals, so we don't have to waste time shopping for food. *Unless* the food shopping is part of our recreational program, and we stroll down Madison Avenue in search of the greengrocer with the perfect chanterelle or the fish market with the first shad roe of the season.

Every now and then, we spend an entire day in bed, reading, watching old movies on television, napping, drinking champagne. (My friend Kate Rand Lloyd, editor-at-large of *Working Woman* magazine, says we are perfect examples of the importance of her "lying fallow" theory. The best ideas come when you're not trying to hatch them.) These days in bed are as good for our bodies as a week at La Costa. No, maybe that's not true. But they are certainly good for our marriage.

We have "just-the-two-of-us" evenings. We learned this trick from Betty and Ned Prentis. Betty, a renowned dancer, hung up her slippers when she married Ned and joined him at becoming an expert in big-game fishing, big-game hunting, and world-class croquet.

Michael stopped in unexpectedly one evening at their New York townhouse to pick up a croquet mallet Ned had selected for him. Betty was in a dinner gown, Ned in black tie. A bottle of champagne was chilling in a bucket, next to a large pot of Beluga caviar.

Michael assumed he had stumbled into the beginning of a formal party, and apologized. Betty and Ned reassured him. They were having one of their "just-the-two-of-us" evenings.

Michael and I don't dress up. And we are more apt to have scrambled eggs than caviar. We love fixing dinner and taking trays to eat in bed. We use them so often that Jenny Maas makes bed trays an almost annual Christmas gift.

From the beginning of our marriage, we've had a "no picking" clause. We ignore small flaws. Michael never refills ice trays, for instance. He puts them carefully back into the freezer, empty. I am a compulsive cleaner. When Mabe is not around on weekends, lack of order makes me wild. So I don't grumble over empty ice trays and Michael shuts his ears to the sound of the vacuum early Sunday mornings.

We *never* criticize each other in public. (Our definition of "public" is anyone other than the two of us.) We are quick to praise each other, slow to pan.

Michael has a special knack for making me feel good about myself. At the kickoff dinner for Bucknell University's 58-million-dollar campaign, I, as the only woman officer of the board, was the sole woman at the dais. Michael was seated out somewhere in the vastness of Davis Gym. Shortly after the soup, he climbed the dais to whisper in my ear, "You look positively radiant." He certainly made me feel that way.

At a big New York cocktail party, Michael was deep in conversation with actress Joan Fontaine. They spoke for at least half an hour, and Michael seemed to be doing most of the talking. Later Joan came over to me. "Your husband thinks you're pretty special," she reported. "All he wanted to talk about was *you*."

Michael and I are both devoted to a number of special interests. In addition to the Bucknell and Fordham boards, I spend time for Advertising Women of New York and Women in Communications. Michael is on the board of the Boy Scouts and the Building Congress, and a member of the Women's Financial Association of New York, a group with clout. Michael is one of the few men to be tapped for admission to this select association. Whenever he teases me about how he never expected to sleep next to a president, I retort that I am always surprised to wake up beside a financial woman!

Michael and I don't usually accompany each other on business trips, usually because they are brief. I don't expect Michael will want to travel with me on overnight trips to Hartford or St. Louis. He feels the same way.

For longer trips, especially those that involve an attractive destination, we make the decision on an *ad hoc* basis. Once, when Michael flew to a meeting in Los Angeles, I left a sales meeting in Utah to join him for a weekend at L'Ermitage. It was bliss. We never left our room.

One couple who travel together often on business trips are Jock and Elly Elliot. Jock, chairman emeritus of Ogilvy & Mather, and one of nine living members of the Advertising Hall of Fame, circumnavigates the globe almost annually to visit dozens of the agency's international offices. Jock tries to adjust *his* schedule and Elly tries to adjust *hers* so they can travel together. (She's a board member of Celanese and New York Hospital and former chairman of the board of Barnard, just to name a few activities.)

Elly not only spends time with the wives of top management—still an important ritual in many countries—but also makes it her special business to talk to women working in the advertising agencies. She has become an authority on the status of working women everywhere.

"It's great fun to see the world," Elly says. "And these trips last for *weeks!* That's far too long for Jock and me to be apart." Hear, hear!

I *always* join Michael for the annual convention of The New York State Building Employers Association. It's *always* held in a warm spot toward the end of January. The men convene mornings, play golf afternoons; the women gather on the beach.

Part of the fun is spending a few days with two of the men who run New York City: John J. Collins and Charles Schaffner. Jack Collins, who was General Manager for Buildings Management and Construction, New York Telephone, is also chairman of the Business Labor Coalition of New York, on whose board Charlie also serves. (Charlie is executive vice president of Syska & Hennessy, the world's largest consulting engineering firm.) Together with Tex Jones, former publisher of The *Daily News*, Jack and Charlie are tackling the biggest problems facing New York City, including mass transit, energy, Times Square, housing, and zoning.

Jack and Phyllis Collins are perfect examples of clients who have become dear friends. Jack is known to me as Sean the Incorrigible. I gave him that nickname one night at Four Seasons. It was my birthday, and Jack handed me an elegantly wrapped package. To my horror, shared by the waiters who were watching, it turned out to be a gallon of gin! Further examination revealed that the gin was water, with two goldfish swimming in it.

Six months later I retaliated by having a plane circle Jack's country club pulling a banner reading: COLLINS IS INCORRIGIBLE. He called that evening to report that everybody in Long Island had seen that plane, and warn me to be on guard for *his* revenge.

All in all, the key to the happy marriage Michael and I enjoy in the midst of our busy careers is *sharing*.

About a dozen years after we were married, I decided to convert from being a "sort of Presbyterian" to Roman Catholicism. Michael was born and raised a Catholic, as were our children. When asked by the curious why I converted, I usually reply offhandedly, "Well, just in case there is a separate Heaven for Catholics, I didn't want

Michael over in his with some gorgeous blonde." The truth is that we were sharing everything else in life, and I wanted to share that part, too.

In 1982, Michael and I celebrated our twenty-fifth wedding anniversary with a nuptial Mass at our church, St. Thomas More, the same church where Kate and Jenny had been baptized. Hugh Carey read from Genesis, Peter Maas read from The New Testament, and my sister Susan Weston read the Twenty-third Psalm. My cup runneth over.

Then our friend and pastor, Monsignor James Wilders, spoke of our marriage and our careers. Michael, the brilliant, successful architect. Jane, the advertising woman who never let a client down.

I started violently in my pew, and turned to Dolores, who was sitting just behind me. "Did we get that ad out to the *Times* before closing?"

Michael thought I was suddenly overcome by emotion, and put his arm around me. "Are you okay?" he asked. "Are you happy?"

Dolores gave me the thumbs-up signal. The ad was delivered on time.

I turned to Michael. "Absolutely, perfectly happy, darling."

And I am.

Index

ABC, 40
Abraham, F. Murray, 71–72
Abraham & Straus, 197
Absinthe House, 25–26
Advertising Hall of Fame, 215
Advertising Women of New
York, 214
Adweek, 183
Ah, Wilderness! (O'Neill), 17
Aim, 54
Alka-Seltzer, 100
Allen, Fred, 27
Allentuck, Max, 25
All-Japan Feminist Association,
134
Amadeus, 72
American Express, 74, 80, 92
American Invsco, 143
*The Amy Vanderbilt Book of
Etiquette,* 145
Annie, 127
Associated Press, 32
Atsumi, Ikuko, 134, 135

Bach, Julian, 78
Baer, Henry, 195
Baer, Marianne, 81
Baker, George, 26
Baker, Wilder, 47
Baldrige, Letitia (Tish), 138, 145,
147

Barnard College, 215
Barrault, Jean-Louis, 20
Barris, Chuck, 40
Barzman, Alan, 94
Batter Fry, 75
BBDO/West, 151
Beber, Joyce, 177
Beber, Silverstein & Partners,
163, 181
Beowulf, 18
Bergen, Polly, 114
Berko, Paul, 199
Berman, Eleanor, 46
Berns, Jerry, 8
Bernstein, Leonard, 142
Betancourt, John, 201
*Better Brochures, Catalogs and
Mailing Pieces* (Maas), 123, 175
Beverly Hills Hotel, 94
Bic, 100, 118
Bitros, Jim, 176
Blair, 198, 199
Blanchard, Leslie, 174
Blaney, John (Black Jack), 70, 98
Blaney, Megan, 70
Blaney, Natalie, 70
Blass, Bill, 168
Bodiker, Susan, 193
Bogarde, Dirk, 84
Bogart, Humphrey, 14
Borghese, Chuck, 194

Bounty, 68, 104
Bourke-White, Margaret, 22
Bower, Marvin, 78
Bowery Savings Bank, 79
Boyd, Betsy, 130
Brady, Nick, 148
Braniff, 111, 118
Braun, Dave, 73, 91
British Travel, 47
Browning, Robert, 75
Brown University, 93, 95
Brugnolatti, Louie (Lulu), 32–33
Brynner, Yul, 126, 127
The Bucknellian, 17, 18
Bucknell University, 8–9, 16–19,
  123, 197, 214
Building Congress, 178, 196, 215
Burke Recall Test, 64–65, 89,
  105, 110
Business Council for the Equal
  Rights Amendment, 114
Business Labor Coalition of New
  York, 216
Butler, Roger, 152
Butler Aviation, 8, 140

Calvert, Dale, 199
Capp, Al, 26
Carey, Chris, 147
Carey, Edward, 148
Carey, Hugh, 118, 120, 127,
  139–148, 160–161, 196, 217
Carlton House, 171
Carter, President and Mrs., 114
Casablanca, 7, 14
Catholic Charities, 121
Catlett, Mary Jo, 63
CBS, 15, 32
Centers, Lu, 202
Charmin, 68, 104
Chase, Mary, 5, 191, 192
Children of a Lesser God, 21
A Chorus Line, 127
Christian, Linda, 28
Christian Association, 18

Christina, Marisa, 198
Churchill, Winston, 39
Claudel, Paul, 20
Clifford, Charlie, 179
Coast, 106–107
Cobra perfume, 159
Coco, Jimmy, 67
Cohoes Specialty Store, 197–198
Colbert, Terry, 141, 166
Colgate, 107
Collier's magazine, 25–26
Collins, John J., 216
Collins, Phyllis, 216
Colman, Jerry, 192
Come Fare Publicita, 193
Comet, 104
Command Airways, 133
Compton, 121
Condon, Richard, 25
Confessions of an Advertising Man
  (Ogilvy), 49, 51, 72–73, 78
Conrad, Sue, 91
A Cool, Clear Death (Halleran),
  200
Cooper, Gary, 86, 88, 91
Cornell University, 20–21
Costello, Dick, 47
Couch, Suzan, 93, 94, 96
Country Time, 68
Cox, Bob, 99
Crocodile Crayons, 159
Cronyn, Hume, 127
Crossland, Felicity, 87, 88–89, 92
Cunard, 56

Dahl, Ludy, 87
Dahl, Olivia, 88
Dahl, Ophelia, 87
Dahl, Roald, 84–92
Dahl, Tessa, 87, 90
Dahl, Theo, 87
Daniels, Judy, 138
Daniels, William, 42
Davidson, Gordon, 21
Davis, Ed, 17, 25, 39, 41

Day, Doris, 158–159
Death in the Afternoon
  (Hemingway), 36
Death of a Salesman, 42
DeCoo, George, 46
DeLuca, Ron, 188, 195
Dempsey, Anne, 184
Dempster, George, 139, 198
Dentsu, 78, 136–137
Dewhurst, Colleen, 42
DeWitt, George, 16, 28, 31, 32,
  34
Dijon, University of, 20
DiMaggio, Joe, 79
Dixon, Carole, 10, 178–179, 211
Donnellon, Kenn, 198–199
Doremus, 49
Dougherty, Phil, 3, 47, 174,
  182–183, 198
Dove, 54, 61–62, 63, 65, 66, 67,
  74, 79, 149
Dowling, Bill, 163–164, 172
Doyle, William, 119, 122, 123,
  126, 128, 131
Doyle Dane Bernbach, 43, 107
Drackett Co., 67, 68, 70, 71
Dragoti, Stan, 126
Drano, 53, 63, 67, 104–105
Driscoll, Brother, 142
Duncan, Sandy, 131
Dyce, Carmen (Mabe), 206–209
Dyson, John, 119, 128, 131

Earth Harvest breads, 187
Economos, Jim, 195
Ehrlich, Aaron, 104, 192, 197
Eklund, Coy, 114
Elephant Premium Floppy Discs,
  155
Elizabeth, Queen, 140
Elliott, Audrey, 69
Elliott, Elly, 69, 215
Elliott, Jock, 50, 55, 68, 98,
  215
Elson, Paul, 176

Equitable Life, 114
"Esso World Theater," 40, 42
Evans, Nick, 70
Excelsior Hotel, 125
Executive House, 35, 36
Ex-Lax, 68
Exxon, 40

A Face in the Crowd, 87
Fagan, Patrick, 12, 188, 195, 198
Fairbanks, Douglas Jr., 161
Favor, 107
Ferguson, Jim, 83
Field, Clifford, 47, 50
Finley, Kumble, Wagner, Heine,
  Underberg, Manley & Casey,
  196, 208
Fisher, Maria, 183
Fitzgerald, Pegeen, 138
Flynn, Carol, 197
Fontaine, Frankie, 104–105
Fontaine, Joan, 214
Foote, Cone & Belding, 52
Ford, George, 37
Forde, Larry, 196
Fordham University, 197, 214
Forty One Madison, 10, 178,
  179
Foster Wheeler, 185
The Fountainhead, 86
Four Seasons, 113, 216
Francis, Arlene, 157, 158
Francke, Linda Bird, 52
Freberg, Stan, 95
Fredericks, Charlie, 47, 80, 102,
  110
Frosch, Aaron, 66
Fry, Christopher, 41

Gage & Tollner, 211
Gardiner, Mark, 195
Gardiner, Wally, 195
Gauff, Susan, 13
Gelb, Alan, 196
General Foods, 51, 65, 72, 73,

General Foods *(continued)* 74–76, 82, 84, 86, 91, 107, 157, 158, 200

The Ghost Writer (Roth), 17

The Gin Game, 127

Gionfriddo, Gwen, 192

Girl Scout Council of Greater New York, 197

Glade, 54, 81

Glaser, Milton, 3, 120

Jackie Gleason Show, 104

Gleem, 101

Glenn, Annie, 29

Glenn, John, 28–30

Goff cat food, 159

Goluskin, Norman, 47

Gomes, Greg, 201

"The Gong Show," 40

Good Housekeeping, 1

Goodhue, Ruth, 22, 23

Gottlieb, Blanche, 196

Gouletas, Evangeline (Engie), 143–146, 161

Gouletas, Nicholas, 143, 148

Gouletas, Victor, 143

Governor's Committee on Scholastic Achievement, 9, 195–196

The Graduate, 42

Graham, Katherine, 111

Graves, Robert, 40

Graybar Building, 165, 166, 173, 180, 181

Grayson, Gene, 44, 48, 66, 71, 79, 98, 150, 151

Grease, 127

Griner, Norman, 86, 88

Haber, Marty, 196

Hackett, Buddy, 25

Halleran, Judith (Jude), 200, 201

Halleran, Tucker, 200

Hamilton, Margaret, 68

Hardy, Robin, 40

Harley Hotel, 163, 164, 167, 175, 176

Harley Middletowne, 167

Harley Windsor, 167

Harrington, Pat, 94

Hart, Kitty Carlisle, 142, 161, 196

Hartford, University of, 200

Hartigan, Marikay, 49

Hassett, William D. Jr., 131, 139

Hassler Hotel, 124

The Hasty Heart, 87

Hayakawa, Sussue, 40

Heekin, John, 70

Hello, Dolly!, 63

Helmsley, Harry, 160, 161–162, 165, 166, 170

Helmsley, Leona Mindy Roberts Rosenthal, 1, 160–181

Helmsley Palace, 162–163, 164, 171, 177, 180, 181

Helmsley-Spear, 165

Hess, Leon, 161

HFD, 10

HLW, 1

Hochstein, Peter, 49, 82, 153

Hodges, Eddie, 29, 30

Hoff, Ron, 52, 59–60

Hogan, Don, 122–123

A Hole in the Head, 29

Hope, Bob, 100

Horst, 146

Hospitality Inns, 167

Hotel Sales Management Association, 134, 176

Houghton, David X., 48

Houghton, Francis X., 46–47

Hoving, Walter, 161

How to Advertise (Roman and Maas), 6, 78, 97, 100, 108, 123, 134, 193

The Hucksters, 16

Hud, 87

Hughes, Colette, 194

Hughes, Emmet, 24

Huxtable, Ada Louise, 138
Hyatt Hotel, 166

Ikard, Todd, 5, 191
"I Love New York" campaign,
116–148
Imperial Schrade, 10, 54, 188,
195, 199
In Harm's Way, 87
In Search of Excellence, 75
International Paper, 106
Iona College, 142
Irish, Judson, 60
Italian Shoe Center, 193, 194
Italian Trade Commission, 193

Jackson, Dee, 166
Jackson, Glenda, 84
Jacobs, Fred, 129, 130, 145
James, Bob, 47
Jean Louis, 169
Jenkins, Jeannie, 210, 211
John Loves Mary, 86
Johnson, Arte, 71
Johnson, Sam, 81
Johnson Wax Co., 79, 80–81, 107
Jones, Abe, 47
Jones, Tex, 216
Jordan, John, 11, 182, 184, 185
Jueneman, Mrs. Gus, 32
Julia, 168, 173, 174, 175

Kalfus, Mel, 192, 193, 194
Kanner, Bernice, 69
Karmen, Steve, 119, 142
Keil, Reuben, 31, 32
Kelley, Brendan, 155
Kellogg, 25
Kennedy, Caroline, 41
Kennedy, Jacqueline, 41
Kennedy, John F., 41
Kennedy, John Jr., 41
Keown, Ian, 45–46
Kerner, Elaine, 139

Kershaw, Andrew, 77, 79, 82, 92,
98, 103
The King and I, 126, 127
Kir, Canon, 20
The Kite, 40
Kiya, 136
KLM Royal Dutch Airline, 46
Koch, Ed, 127, 146
Korda, Reva, 48, 68
Kovi, Paul, 113
Kriendler, Robert, 7
Krupsak, Mary Anne, 127
Kugelman, Arthur, 103–104,
105, 106, 107, 108, 109, 110
Kumble, Peggy Vandervoort, 208
Kumble, Steve, 195, 196, 208
Kurland, Mort, 209

The Lady's Not for Burning (Fry),
41
Langella, Frank, 127–128
Lasso, 185
"Laugh-In," 71
Lawrence, Bert, 40
Lawrence, Harding, 112
Lawrence, Mary Wells, 102,
110–114, 118, 145, 166
Lawson, Tom, 47
League of New York Theaters
and Producers, 126
League of Women Voters, 114
Lee, Trudi, 30–32
Leiby, Ken, 79
Leiby, Mary, 79
Lesser, Mike, 47
Lever Brothers, 61, 65, 67, 107
Rick Levine Productions, 155
Levolor, 6, 11, 12, 14, 184
Levy, Norman, 108
Liberati, Gianluigi, 194
Life, 21
"Li'l Abner," 26
Litwin, Frank, 192
Lloyd, Kate Rand, 213

Look, 39
Loren, Sophia, 105–106
Lorre, Peter, 14
Luce, Claire Booth, 22
Luce, Henry, 21–22, 24
Luce, Henry III, 23
Luckman, Jim, 94
Luna, 211

Jane Maas, Inc., 166, 167, 176,
   178, 179, 181, 184
Maas, Jenny, 12, 41, 57, 66, 75,
   148, 155–156, 204, 205
Maas, Kate, 12, 38, 57, 66, 68, 75,
   148, 156, 204, 205
Maas, Michael, 11, 14, 35–37, 57,
   58, 66, 67, 91, 101–102, 106,
   113, 130, 138–139, 141, 148,
   156, 160–161, 165, 167,
   179–180, 183, 196–197,
   203–204, 205, 209–210,
   213–217, 275
Maas, Peter, 26, 35, 139, 217
MacGraw, Ali, 106
Macy's, 48, 93
The Madwoman of Chaillot, 17
Magazine Publishers' Association,
   56–57
I. Magnin, 189
Malden, Karl, 92
The Manhattans, 142
Man in the Gray Flannel Suit, 16
Mantle, Mickey, 141
Manufacturer's Hanover
   Corporate Challenge Race,
   201–202
Margittai, Tom, 113
Marie (Maas), 26
Mark Taper Forum, Los Angeles,
   21
Marshall, Bob, 47
Martin, John, 47
Matschulat, Natel, 131, 142
Maxim, 54, 73, 74, 83–84, 89,
   105

Maxwell House, 51, 54, 68, 77,
   91
Mahoney, David, 161
Mayor (Koch), 146
Mazzola, John, 162
McGraw-Hill, 185
McPherson, Aimee Semple, 27
Menaker, Fran, 12
Merrill Lynch, 52, 151, 152, 154
Meyer, Sandra, 74
Mies Van der Rohe, Ludwig, 51
Milky Way, 150
Miller, Bill, 92
Miller, Elliott, 5, 192
Miller, Mitch, 30
Miss America Pageant, 40
Monsanto, 11, 14, 185
Montreal Canadiens, 8
Moon, Sun Yung, 119
Morgan, Henry, 25
Moseley, Chris, 200
Moss, Charlie, 99, 100, 101,
   102–103, 110, 111, 112, 116,
   118, 126
Muller, Frank, 10, 184, 185
Muller Jordan Weiss, 3, 4, 5–6, 9,
   11, 103, 104, 159, 174, 176,
   183, 185–202
Mulligan, Peter, 5, 192
The Music Man, 29
Mussachio, Bob, 129

Namath, Joe, 141
"Name That Tune," 15, 27–35
National Distillers, 79
National Lampoon, 181
National Organization for
   Women, 65, 69
NBC, 39
Neal, Patricia, 83, 84–92, 105
"The Newlywed Game," 40
Newman, Paul, 87
Newsweek, 52
New York Daily News, 181, 216
The New Yorker, 189

New York Helicopter, 198
New York Hospital, 38, 215
New York magazine, 69
New York Merchandise Mart, 10, 178
New York State Building Employers Association, 215–216
New York State "I Love New York" campaign, 116–148
New York State Orchestra, 142
New York State Travel and Vacation Association, 123
New York Telephone, 216
The New York Times, 2, 50, 174, 181, 182
Nixon, Richard, 152

Obiyashi, Michiko, 135, 136
O'Brien, Bess, 211–212
O'Brien, Dennis, 197
O'Brien, Mike, 98
Oedipus Rex (Sophocles), 17
Ogilvy, David, 6, 33, 43–60, 78, 79, 103, 191, 200, 204
Ogilvy, Herta, 58
Ogilvy & Mather, 33, 43–57, 83, 84, 100, 101, 151, 154, 208, 215
O'Hare, Father, 197
Ohashi, Terue, 135, 136
Old Crow, 79
On Your Toes, 196
Open Pit, 74
Oppenheimer, Judy Jordan, 211
Oppenheimer Fund, 185
Our Town, 17

Page, Shelby, 64
Palmolive, 68
Papert, Fred, 165–166
Papert, Koenig, Lois, 165
Papone, Aldo, 96
Parkinson, Norman (Parks), 167–168

Park Lane Hotel, 161, 163, 164, 167, 168, 177
Parks, Bert, 40
The Patricia Neal Story, 84
Paxinou, Katina, 40
Peck, Mr. & Mrs. Gregory, 161
Peckham, Content, 22
Pepperidge Farm, 54, 68
Phillips, Bill, 47, 51, 83, 98
Pine Valley, 211
Pledge, 107
Plummer, Christopher, 212
Polykoff, Shirley, 138
Power, Tyrone, 28
Powers, Harvey, 17
Prell, 101, 102, 108–109, 111
Prentis, Betty, 213–214
Prentis, Ned, 213–214
Preston, Robert, 25, 29
Price, Steve, 199–200
Procter & Gamble, 65, 70, 97, 99, 101, 104–110, 185
Project Acorn, 75–77

QE II, liner, 56, 61

Radio Advertising Bureau, 95
Raphaelson, Joel, 44, 48, 49
Rather, Dan, 161
Ray, Satyajit, 40
Reagan, Ronald, 86
Reiss, Elaine, 69, 95
Reynolds, Benny, 15
Russell Reynolds Associates, 74
Rich, Adrienne, 134
Richardson, Sir Ralph, 40
Robinson, Dave, 198
Rocky Mountain Ski Association, 80
Rolls-Royce, 50
Roman, Ken, 47, 77, 82, 97, 98, 108, 183, 189, 190, 199
Rooney, Pat, 33
Roosevelt, Franklin D., 140
Roper, Elmo, 37, 41

Rose, Michael, 196
Rosenthal, Jay, 169
Ross, Mark, 86, 88
Roth, Philip, 17
Roundup, 185
Rudin, Jack, 178, 179
Rudin Management, 178, 179

Sabatini's, 124
Sabinson, Harvey, 126
"Sad Sack," 26
Safeguard, 101, 103, 105–106, 108
Safire, William, 64
Sager, Scott, 194
St. Moritz Hotel, 167, 176, 177
St. Regis Hotel, 147, 148
Salter, Harry, 2, 27, 28, 30–31, 34, 35, 39–40
Salter, Roberta Semple, 27, 32, 63
Sanka, 105, 107
Savage, Bob, 47
Savvy, 138
"Scarlet Ribbons," 30
Scavullo, Francesco, 128
Schaffner, Charles, 216
School for Scandal (Sheridan), 17
Schulberg, Jay, 59, 81
Scott, George C., 42
Sears, Roebuck, 54
Seclow, Richard, 47
Seiniger, David, 198
Serpico (Maas), 26
The Shadow Box, 21
Shake 'n Bake, 68, 74
Shell, 106
Shields, Brooke, 169
Sills, Beverly, 131
Silverman, Bruce, 151
Silverman, Jack, 58–59, 150, 151, 158–159
Silvers, Phil, 25, 32
Simpson, Diane, 134–135
Simpson, O. J., 141

Sinatra, Frank, 29, 180, 181
"Sing Along with Mitch," 30
"$64,000 Question," 39
Smith, Smith, Haines, Lundberg & Waehler, 66
Smoke Enders, 82
Society for Savings Bank of Hartford, 1, 3, 4–5, 191–192, 201
Soho Charcuterie, 211
Sojka, Gary, 197
Space Bank, 92
Stapleton, Maureen, 25
Start, 54, 74
Stauderman, Bruce, 157
Stavropoulos, George, 147
Stern, Marty, 117, 118, 131, 183
Stevenson, Adlai, 22, 32
Stewart, George, 166
Stimorol chewing gum, 189
Stone, Mike, 189
"Stop the Camera," 39
"Stop the Music," 27, 40
Stroehmann Bakeries, 1, 7, 104, 186, 198
The Student Prince, 17
Sudden Death Finish (Halleran), 200
Susskind, David, 161
Syska & Hennessy, 216

Tamaru, Hideharu, 78–79
Tanaka, Shoji, 136
Tandy, Jessica, 127
Taster's Choice, 83–84
Tavern on the Green, 127
Taylor, Bill, 92
Taylor, Elizabeth, 66
Theater Now, 17
Tillinghast, Charles, 95
Time Inc., 21, 22, 28, 35
Time, 22, 23, 28, 127
Tishman, John, 196
Touffou, 57–58
Trachtenberg, Marty, 200

Trachtenberg, Steve, 200
Trahey, Jane, 79
Trapp, Ray, 47
Trigere, Pauline, 168
Tsai, Gerry, 161
Tuchman, Barbara, 138
Tumi, 179
TWA, 57, 80
Twelfth Night, 17, 21
"Twenty-One," TV show, 39
"21" Club, 4, 7, 96, 113, 140

Uggams, Leslie, 30

The Valachi Papers (Maas), 26
Valentino, 168
Van Doren, Mark, 39
Vanish, 70, 71
Villard House, 164
Von Furstenberg, Diane, 168

Wagner, Phyllis Cerf, 161, 162,
    167, 174
Wagner, Robert, 161, 167, 195
Walden Farms, 7, 199
Wallace, Mike, 161
The Wall Street Journal, 128
Walters, Barbara, 138
Washington Post, 111
Wasserstein, Wendy, 181
Waters, George, 92, 93
Wayne, John, 87
Weiss, Andy, 12, 184, 188, 195
Weiss, Dave, 47, 73, 88
Weiss, Marilyn, 184
Wells, Rich, Greene, 3, 4, 97–98,
    99, 100, 102, 110, 116–117,
    121, 127, 128, 129, 145, 166

Werblin, Sonny, 161
Western Union, 146–147
Weston, Susan, 174, 217
Weston Bakeries Limited, 186
Whistle, 72
White, Theodore, 24
Wilders, James, 217
The Wiz, 127
Women and Power (Trahey), 79
Women in Communications, 138,
    214
Women's Financial Association of
    New York, 215
Women's Forum, 69
Woolf, Virginia, 18
WordPerfect software, 193
Working Woman, 213
Wright, Bill, 54
Wright, Frank Lloyd, 81, 198
Wygant, Pete, 7, 8, 10, 186–187,
    188
Wyse, Lois, 184
Wyse Advertising, 184

Young, Robert, 105
"Yours for a Song," 40

Zahn, Dolores Coyne, 3–4, 5, 8,
    9, 10, 58, 120–121, 133, 141,
    166, 178, 183, 190–191, 200,
    201, 217
Zahn, Mary, 121
Zahn, Norman, 121, 166, 200
Zarem, Bobby, 127
Zimmerman, Sanford, 197, 198
Zorn, Marty, 195, 199
Zuretti, Chuck, 168